Evalua

Professor Harry S

Doctor Juanita El

The Chartered Institute of Personnel and Development is the leading publisher of books and reports for personnel and training professionals, students, and all those concerned with the effective management and development of people at work. For full details of all our titles, please contact the Publishing Department:

Tel: 020 8263 3387
Fax: 020 8263 3850

E-mail: publish@cipd.co.uk

To view and purchase the full range of CIPD publications:
www.cipd.co.uk/bookstore

Evaluating Human Capital

Professor Harry Scarbrough

Warwick Business School, University of Warwick

Doctor Juanita Elias

BRASS Research Centre, University of Cardiff

© Chartered Institute of Personnel and Development 2002

First published 2002
Reprinted 2004

Cover design by Curve
Designed and typeset by Beacon GDT
Printed in Great Britain by Short Run Press

British Library Cataloguing in Publication Data
A catalogue record for this book is available from the British Library

ISBN 0 85292 974 9

Chartered Institute of Personnel and Development,
CIPD House, Camp Road, London SW19 4UX

Tel: 020 8971 9000
Fax: 020 8263 3333
Website: www.cipd.co.uk

Incorporated by Royal Charter. Registered charity no. 1079797.

Contents

Foreword

The issue of human capital has dominated the business agenda for some time. The old adage 'People are our most important asset' has been a stock phrase for many a company director and annual report. However when we look more closely at the basis on which these same people make important business decisions we find this phrase to be little more than empty rhetoric. In reality few business decisions are made with any real knowledge and understanding of the contribution of people.

How many companies are taken over, only to find the very reason they were attractive to an outside bidder – the talent of their people and hence their ability to innovate and develop creative solutions – vanishes? Poor management and unrealistic opinions about the needs and expectations of people can damage this vital resource overnight. How much valuable talent is wasted by an organisation's inability to leverage that talent by persuading individuals to share their skills and competence freely? In the knowledge-driven economy to which the UK aspires, people are both the most valuable and also the most volatile organisational asset.

Why are such obviously negative strategies allowed to develop? Undoubtedly because measuring the contribution of people and generating data which can be set alongside other data used in business decisions has to date proved a thorny issue. 'What gets measured matters', is never more true than in terms of business decision-making.

The Chartered Institute of Personnel and Development has been working since 1997 in the area of investigating the link between the way in which people are managed and business performance. This report forms another vital piece of the jigsaw that we are trying to put together offering better understanding, knowledge and information in this area.

We initiated this work on human capital with the following aims:

1. to create a framework of shared understanding about the nature of human capital

2. to identify some common principles for the analysis of human capital

3. to identify how we might move forward in developing a coherent set of measures that may be applied to the impact of human capital in a variety of circumstances.

We were never under any illusion that it would be possible to generate a universal formula for the measurement of human capital or that this six-month exploratory study would provide all the answers. However we hoped it would be possible to define some common principles on which to move forward to develop a range of measures that would ultimately enable companies to gather better-quality information on the contribution of their human capital.

The final outcome of the work exceeds all our expectations. It provides a solid foundation on which to build to develop measures to evaluate human capital, and frameworks for reporting these measures.

The first half of this report reviews the extensive body of literature in the human capital area. The second part reviews the experiences of a number of organisations that are making real and deliberate efforts to better understand the contribution of their people to the success of their business. A number of common themes and principles have been identified, as have a number of barriers and reasons why managers do not make more effort to evaluate human capital.

Harry Scarbrough and Juanita Elias have managed to make sense of an extensive and complex body of literature which has given rise to numerous theories and perspectives. By relating this to actual practice they are able to identify the significant issues for managers who want to make serious attempts to better understand their human capital.

This report complements the other studies that the CIPD has published in the area which have all identified the problems of the measurement of the contribution of people to the business as key to understanding the link between people management and business success more clearly.

Harry and Juanita make a number of recommendations at the end of the report to move thinking forward in this area. The CIPD is already making strenuous efforts to develop tools and processes to enable organisations to better evaluate their human capital and communicate this to those who make the most important decisions about the long-term performance and viability of organisations.

Angela Baron
Adviser, Organisation and Resourcing
Chartered Institute of Personnel and Development

Executive Summary

This report contains the findings of an exploratory six-month study, commissioned by the CIPD, of the ways in which a small sample of UK-based firms evaluate their human capital. It aims to advance our understanding of both the opportunities and challenges confronting firms that wish to develop a more systematic approach to the measurement, management and development of the people that they employ.

The need for more systematic approaches is underlined by the growing disparity between the contribution that human capital makes to firm performance and the existing means of identifying and valuing that contribution. As numerous studies have underlined, the economic conditions created by globalisation and the advent of new technologies have combined to make human capital and other intangible assets the major drivers of economic competitiveness. The increasingly critical role of these factors, however, has not been matched by advances in management and accounting practices that would allow that role to be properly reflected in management decision-making and the operation of capital markets. Without advances in the *internal* measurement and reporting of human capital, management are unable to fully recognise the value of their employees' competencies and commitment for business performance. Investments in training and development are viewed narrowly as costs, and the contribution of key skills risks being lost through mergers and restructuring. Without advances in the *external* reporting of human capital, capital markets are unable to allocate capital efficiently to firms whose principal assets are not reflected in their balance sheets.

The study sought to address these issues by relating the existing theories and models for the evaluation of human capital to actual practices in 10 major firms based in the UK, drawn from a variety of sectors. The major findings of this study are summarised below, first in relation to the managerial challenges posed by human capital, and second in relation to current practice, as revealed by our study.

Human capital – the challenge

1. The concept of human capital is most usefully viewed as a bridging concept – that is, it defines the link between HR practices and business performance in terms of assets rather than business processes.

2. Human capital is a precarious asset. This is because the potential mobility of individual employees undermines the firm's ability to derive full benefit from the skills they bring to the organisation.

3. Human capital is a paradoxical asset. The same qualities that make it crucial to competitiveness – flexibility, mobility, inimitability – make it difficult to measure and manage.

4. Human capital is context-dependent – that is, the competencies and commitment which create value in one context may be worthless in another. The value-creating effect of human capital is highly specific.

Current practices

1. Our case-study firms were making significant improvements in the internal reporting of human capital. None, however, was concerned to incorporate human capital in their external reporting. Their efforts focused on internal evaluation and reporting for managerial purposes.

2. In a number of cases, the evaluation of human capital took place in the context of the firm's adoption of the 'balanced scorecard' approach to business strategy.

3. The case firms did not use the term 'human capital' but had developed their own criteria of competence which were linked to the wider business environment they faced, and the values that they sought to apply to that environment. In this way, they overcame some of the problems associated with more generic measures of human capital.

4. The drive to develop a better understanding of the firm's human capital came from a variety of factors, including: major organisational changes; developments in HR practice through greater professionalism; and the problems of management and succession planning in increasingly global businesses.

5. The advantages that these firms identified from the evaluation of human capital were equally varied, and included: aligning people strategy to business strategy; evaluating the feasibility of business plans in terms of employee capability; and identifying skills gaps.

6. While some firms focused much of their effort on the 'war for talent' – that is, recruitment and retention of a small group of employees – others sought to highlight the contribution made by the workforce as a whole.

7. Interest in the evaluation of human capital was linked to the nature of employees' contribution to the business. Interest seemed to be greatest where employee competencies were a moderately important or ambiguous factor in competitive success.

Overall, our study found that there was no 'holy grail' in the evaluation of human capital – no single measure that was independent of context and that could accurately represent the impact of employee competencies and commitment on business performance. This is not to suggest that metrics and other forms of information are irrelevant to the task of managing human capital. Rather, our study suggests that such information flows need to be embedded in wider processes of dialogue and exchange which, over time, enhance the knowledge of managers, employees and investors as to the value of human capital. In short, measures are less important than the activity of measuring – of continuously developing and refining our understanding of the productive role of human capital within particular settings. By embedding such activities in management practices, and linking them to the business strategy of the firm, firms may yet be capable of developing a more coherent and ultimately strategic approach to one of the most powerful, if elusive, drivers of competitiveness.

1 | Introduction

This report contains the findings of an exploratory six-month study of the ways in which a small sample of UK-based firms evaluate their human capital. It aims to advance our understanding of both the opportunities and the challenges confronting firms that wish to develop a more systematic approach to the competencies of the people that they employ. This introduction thus proceeds as follows: the first section provides a brief introduction to the current context for the debate on human capital; the second section highlights the different definitions and characteristics of human capital; the third section outlines some of the possible challenges and opportunities that confront firms seeking to evaluate the human capital of their employees, including the issues of reporting and measuring human capital; the fourth section goes on to review the managerial implications of human capital; and the final section outlines the research study and the way in which we have operationalised the evaluation of human capital within that study.

The context for this study is defined by the emergence of the knowledge economy. As numerous studies have underlined, the new economic conditions exhibit several features which place human capital at the centre of debates on competitiveness:

1. Globalisation, coupled with the liberalisation of trade and the spread of education, has an equalising effect on competition. Geographical location may no longer offer privileged access to markets or finance capital. Product and process technologies are highly mobile across international boundaries (Leadbeater, 2000).

2. Competitiveness depends on access to assets that cannot be readily imitated by competitors (Barney, 1991).

3. For advanced economies, 'competitiveness increasingly comes from 'distinctive assets which can be used to generate high value products. These assets are know-how, skills, creativity and talent' (Leadbeater, 2000: 5). One recent estimate suggests that US industrial firms are now investing as much in intangible assets such as R&D and training as they do in physical plant and equipment (Lev, 1998).

If the emergence of the knowledge economy is not to be stalled by outdated management practices, however, there is an urgent need to develop more effective ways of evaluating the intangible assets possessed by firms, chief amongst them being human capital. The UK Government's recognition of the increasing urgency of this need was expressed in the 1999 White Paper on 'Government and business in the knowledge driven economy'. This argued that:

In the increasingly global economy of today, we cannot compete in the old way. Capital is mobile, technology can migrate quickly and goods can be made in low cost countries and shipped to developed markets. British business must compete by exploiting capabilities that its competitors cannot easily match or imitate. These distinctive capabilities are not raw materials, land or access to cheap labour. They must be knowledge, skills and creativity, which help create high productivity business processes and high value goods and services. That is why we will only compete successfully in future if we create an economy that is genuinely 'knowledge driven'.

The implication of this view is the need for systematic assessment of the intangible assets of firms:

The Government would like to see better guidance for companies of all sizes on assessing the strengths and weaknesses of their intangible assets, including the skills of their people. (our emphasis)

The attention that government and business are increasingly paying to human capital reflects this broader concern with intangible assets in the knowledge economy. Human capital is repeatedly identified as one of the most important intangible assets in the knowledge economy. The increasing importance of such assets poses a major challenge to existing methods of accounting and valuation. The scale of that challenge is reflected in the size of the gap between the value of a company's tangible assets in its balance sheet and its stock market value. This so-called 'market-to-book ratio' is especially high for knowledge-intensive firms and service businesses that are especially reliant on human capital. A survey of mergers and acquisitions in the USA over the period 1981 to 1993 found that the mean ratio of the price of acquisition to the book value was 4.4, with a ratio of over 10 for high-tech companies (Bradley, 1997). Thus, for some firms, the tangible assets identified on the balance sheet have come to represent only a fraction of their stock market valuation or their value to other firms. The remainder is attributed to the intangible assets provided by brands, R&D and employees. This growing disparity between market and book values not only reflects the growing importance of intangible assets; it also dramatically exposes the limitations of traditional accounting practices in identifying and measuring the value-adding elements of the firm.

The arguments for evaluating human capital and other intangible assets range from the broad macro-economic advantages to specific managerial benefits in the area of HRM and HRD (Butler *et al*, 2002). While the managerial benefits are discussed in more detail below, it is worth noting that there are important economic policy gains to be derived from the measurement of intangible assets. In particular, it is argued that such measurement should increase the efficiency of capital markets and reduce their volatility. As Bassi *et al* argue:

The decrease in the predictive validity of reported earnings and equity values, based on generally accepted accounting standards, is of more than academic interest. (p. 366)

As they note, the absence of forward-looking information about intangible assets contributes to volatility in capital markets (consider, for example, the spurious valuations of firms that emerged during the 'dot com' bubble). This raises the cost of capital for everyone, but particularly for knowledge-intensive firms. At the same time, the lack of accepted measures of the value of intangible assets probably results in under-investment since there is insufficient attention paid to this area, and managers are less likely to commit time and resources to assets that are difficult to quantify and whose benefits, though significant, may be difficult to specify. Knowledge workers, in particular, may find that their contribution to firm performance is not recognised and rewarded as much as it should be because intangible assets are under-valued or because inappropriate measurement tools are being applied (Leadbeater, 2000).

Defining human capital

As we outline in Chapter 2, the concept of human capital has emerged from a number of debates in different fields. A variety of definitions have been suggested, as outlined in Table 1.

> "...human capital is a precarious organisational asset. This is because the potential mobility of individual employees undermines the firm's ability to derive full benefit from the skills they bring to the organisation."

As we can observe from Table 1, views of human capital revolve around a core specification which is to do with employee competencies (sometimes equated with knowledge), together with the application of such competencies (hence, the inclusion of motivation or commitment in some definitions). In all cases, human capital is viewed as something that employees bring to the organisation, but which is also developed through training and experience within the organisation. Despite its grounding in organisational activity, however, human capital is a precarious organisational asset. This is because the potential mobility of individual employees undermines the firm's ability to derive full benefit from the skills they bring to the organisation. There are many instances of large firms acquiring smaller firms, only to find their most important assets leaving to set up business in competition.

One of the other major barriers to developing more robust measures of human capital is its context-dependent nature. Unlike other forms of capital that can be traded in the marketplace, the value of human capital depends on the context. While this consideration was less important in early macro-economic studies, it is much more significant at organisation level, where we are dealing not with the generality of a whole population but with the skills of specific employee groups. At this level, broad correlations between education levels, experience and economic outcomes cease to operate. The value-creating effect of human capital is highly specific. Competencies that are vital in one firm or one sector may be a liability to another.

At this level, then, human capital is context dependent in several important respects. First, the relative importance of human capital vis-à-vis other tangible and intangible assets varies from one setting to another. Second, particular forms of human capital are themselves context dependent. Such context dependency may operate in a variety of ways. For some skills, it may be the physical or technological environment that is critical. Scribner (1986), for example, found that the practical expertise of a group of inventory takers in a dairy

Table 1 | Definitions of human capital

Source	Definition of human capital
OECD, 1996	Human capital is defined here as the knowledge that individuals acquire during their life and use to produce goods services or ideas in market or non-market circumstances. (OECD, 1996 p.22)
Davenport, 1999	ability (knowledge, skill, talent) + behaviour x effort x time
Stewart, 1997	The capabilities of individuals, teams and communities of practice as they are applied and leveraged by the organisation.
Ulrich, 1998	competence x commitment

> "...in the great majority of UK firms the systems
> for evaluating and reporting human capital are
> either rudimentary or non-existent."

was not transferrable to a classroom context –
their expertise simply disappeared once it was
taken out of the physical and organisational
context defined by their workplace and the
products and processes within it. For others, it may
be aspects of the social or institutional
environment. Certain kinds of professional
expertise, for instance, are valuable only within
very specific institutional settings – the court of
law, the operating theatre – where they are a key
part of an elaborate division of labour.

We can briefly summarise these points by
reviewing the differing managerial perceptions of
key intangible assets across industry sectors, as
highlighted in a recent study (Vance, 2001):

- *Food and drink:* The most important intangible
  asset here was perceived to be the brand.

- *Media:* Brand was again seen as important.
  However, human capital was also emphasised.
  Here the most important form of human
  capital was seen as creative individuals.

- *Software:* Human capital was given great
  importance here along with customer
  relationships. However, managers placed
  greatest importance not on creative individuals
  but on the performance of expert teams.

- *Pharmaceutical sector:* Brand was seen as an
  important asset but only for firms with a strong
  'over the counter' product base. For all firms,
  human capital was seen as important, with
  specific significance attaching to R&D capability
  – the latter being viewed as a product of
  employee competencies and process quality.

- *High technology and telecoms:* Brand was seen
  as an important asset, and in terms of human

capital, R&D was again cited as a key
intangible.

- *Finance:* This sector placed the greatest
  emphasis on customer relationships as the
  most important intangible asset.

- *Defence:* The major intangible here was seen
  as accumulated intellectual property.

These sectoral differences help to underline the
point that while we define human capital in terms
of knowledge or experience, its value is not
intrinsic in the knowledge or experience itself but
rather in the potential of such knowledge to create
value within a particular setting.

Evaluating human capital

Given the sophistication of modern management
techniques, it seems curious, to say the least, that
there should still be a question mark over
managers' ability to adequately understand, value
and deploy what so many experts agree is one of
their major sources of competitive advantage,
namely their people. If firms were as backward in
identifying and reporting on any of the other
major resources at their command, it would be
viewed as nothing short of scandalous. It is
important to bear this point in mind as we proceed
through this report, because the firms that we are
highlighting are, by definition, those that are more
progressive in their approach to human capital. We
should not forget, however, that in the great
majority of UK firms the systems for evaluating
and reporting human capital are either
rudimentary or non-existent.

The reasons for managerial backwardness in this
field relate in large part to the paradoxical
characteristics of human capital. On the one hand,

employee skills and competencies make a critical contribution to business performance. On the other hand, the features which make human capital so critical are the very same features that inhibit evaluation (see Figure 1). Thus, one of the features of human capital that make it so crucial to firm performance is the flexibility and creativity of individuals, their ability to develop skills over time and to respond in a motivated way to different contexts. Much of this depends on the acquisition and application of 'tacit knowledge'; that is, knowledge that we cannot readily articulate but which is acquired through a process of situated learning (Lave and Wenger, 1991).

It follows from this that human capital is to a large extent non-standardised, tacit, dynamic, context dependent and embodied in people. These features provide a competitive advantage because they are causally ambiguous – the relationship between cause and effect is not readily identified. One corollary of these context-dependent and causally ambiguous features is the difficulty that competing firms experience should they try to replicate a firm's human capital base. It is extremely difficult to imitate another firm's

deployment of human capital, and this may provide an enduring source of competitive advantage. On the other hand, while rival firms cannot do this, there is every likelihood that a firm's own managers will not be able to either. Given the role of tacit knowledge, and the context-specific nature of performance, it may be difficult for managers to identify those skills and competencies that are effective in different contexts. And, insofar as they can identify systematic relationships between skills and contexts, this knowledge may be equally tacit on the part of managers themselves – something that they can recognise but which cannot be expressed very readily in terms of explicit frameworks and schemas.

In the subsequent chapters of this report, we shall highlight the implications of this paradox in terms of the related activities of reporting, measuring and managing human capital. We are reviewing these activities separately for analytical purposes, but as our case studies demonstrate, in practice these activities are interdependent and overlap each other.

Figure 1 | Paradox of human capital

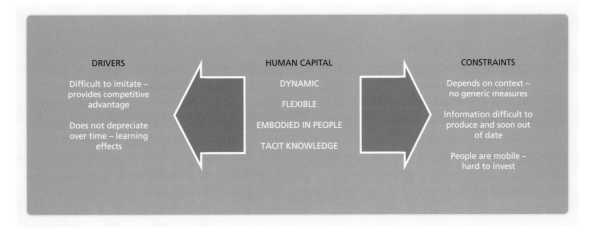

DRIVERS	HUMAN CAPITAL	CONSTRAINTS
Difficult to imitate – provides competitive advantage	DYNAMIC	Depends on context – no generic measures
	FLEXIBLE	Information difficult to produce and soon out of date
Does not depreciate over time – learning effects	EMBODIED IN PEOPLE	
	TACIT KNOWLEDGE	People are mobile – hard to invest

Reporting human capital

There are several major challenges to the reporting of intangible assets such as human capital. The first relates to the scale of intangible assets within advanced economies, the second to the rate of change in business performance arising from the importance of intangible assets, and the third to the nature of intangible assets themselves (Leadbeater, 2000). Such assets are difficult, and sometimes impossible, to trade in markets so market-based valuation is problematic. Moreover, accounting methods are based on historical records of discrete transactions, which provide little understanding of the impact of intangible assets on performance. All of these factors apply *a fortiori* to human capital, which, unlike other forms of capital, cannot be bought and sold as an asset of the firm (Bassi *et al*, 2000). This means that unlike other assets, human capital is not reported in the financial accounts of the firm. A firm's human capital can be reflected in its internally generated 'goodwill' figure, but cannot figure on its balance sheet. Thus, only the costs – and not the benefits – of developing human capital are reported, creating a very lop-sided view of its impact.

The problems of overcoming these barriers to the reporting of human capital can be partially overcome by developing in-house reporting systems. These may avoid the need to link human capital directly to financial valuations by developing a specialised system of information under the aegis of the HR function. As we note in subsequent chapters, the development of internal reporting of human capital through systems developed by the HR function does avoid these accounting barriers. On the other hand, such systems may be restricted in their use to the HR function alone, and they do not address the problem of external reporting of human capital.

Outside of a few well-publicised firms, none of them based in the UK, the external reporting of human capital is of negligible importance in current accounting practice. The reasons for this are not hard to find. They relate partly to the problems of measurement and the definition of assets, which we discuss below. Many of the reasons, however, have to do with corporate governance, and, in particular, the relationship between the firm and the investor community. Here, a recent study (Vance, 2001) has found a significant divergence between managers and the investor community in the attention and given importance attached to intangible assets of all kinds. On the one hand, the companies in the survey, almost without exception, viewed their intangible assets as extremely important. On the other hand, the investor community, that is, merchant banks, analysts and fund managers, were generally indifferent or hostile to the notion of intangible assets. As the report noted:

Few City interviewees felt that the difficulties in communicating and measuring value were susceptible to a solution. Many were openly sceptical of the efforts currently under way to improve the measurement and communication of this value. There was certainly marked antipathy to any form of standardised accounting and reporting in this area. (Vance, 2001: 10)

The report claims that the fundamental tenet of the investor community is that 'cash is king'. In other words, the company valuations made by analysts are based largely on the net present value of future cash flows. In the pharmaceuticals sector, for example, the information provided by firms on their R&D pipeline can help to inform estimates of the future cash flows to be expected from individual drugs. When aggregated together, these cash flows help to establish the value of the company as a cash generator. On the other hand, despite this account, other studies suggest that investors are no longer happy to rely on purely financial data, and are taking more account of intangibles in their decision-making rather than less (LeBlanc *et al*, 2000).

Measuring human capital

Sometimes measurement may be a fetish or an end in itself, without reference to any broader objective. However, it can also play a crucial role in developing our knowledge of a phenomenon. As Lord Kelvin once said:

When you can measure what you are speaking about and express it in numbers, you know something about it; but when you cannot measure, when you cannot express it in numbers, your knowledge is of a meagre and unsatisfactory kind. It may be the beginnings of knowledge, but you have scarcely, in your thoughts, advanced to the stage of a science.

As we noted above, many features of both human capital itself and knowledge about human capital make it highly resistant to codification and measurement. Information about employee competencies and commitment is costly and difficult to compile. It quickly goes out of date, and because it is context dependent is difficult to aggregate across contexts (Bassi *et al*, 2000). And then, employees themselves, the people who might contribute most to ensuring the quality of information, are not passive in this process. They may resist being classified in various ways or may seek to manipulate the measurement process.

As Leadbeater notes, these factors raise doubts about the accuracy and validity of measures of human capital. As he notes, such measures

could result in cumbersome inventories which allow managers to manipulate perceptions of intangible values to the detriment of investors. The fact is that too few of these new measures are focused on the way companies create value and make money. (Leadbeater, 2000: 3)

None of these considerations is fatal in itself to the idea of measuring employee competencies. Indeed, as we note below, the development of IT systems may offer some means of addressing these issues. However, their overall effect is to greatly increase the costs of any such exercise. As a result, where measurement of human capital is undertaken at all (outside the macro-level calculations of economists), it occurs within firms where there are specific managerial reasons for doing so. But such efforts are firm specific. No one firm has an interest in producing more generic information that would be valuable across a number of firms or across even a sector. As a result, despite the public good that would arise from the more systematic measurement of human capital – something that all firms might benefit from – there has been little headway in the development of robust measures or a common language that can be reported and used externally (Bassi *et al*, 2000). The development of such a common language may involve regulatory changes, such as the adoption of new accounting standards. Equally, for managerial practices, the spread of techniques through HR and other forms of benchmarking may also be an important factor.

Managing human capital

The management of human capital is obviously linked to the development of reporting and measuring systems for human capital. Without these information flows, and the wider accountabilities they generate, managers would be unable to take human capital factors into account when making decisions. As Mayo puts it, 'managers are conditioned to working with numbers and nothing has a greater impact' (p.9). However, the impact of such systems on management cannot be discussed simply in terms of the 'single loop learning' that increases the efficiency of existing decision-making processes. The more important effect of such flows of information is to promote new forms of knowledge and understanding within organisations – double loop learning, as it were (Argyris, 1977). Thus, in discussing the management of human capital, we need to address the potentially profound implications of the adoption of a human capital perspective on management practice. The scope of such implications is best indicated by considering this proposition: what would happen if top management actually took seriously that discredited cliché 'Our employees are our most important asset'?

To begin at the strategic level, we need to recognise that viewing employees as human capital rather than costs is not just another way of suggesting that their role is critical to business performance. This is something that can be established without reference to the human capital concept. Rather, to say that employees represent human capital is to redefine the relationship between the firm's employment policies and its business performance. Most existing studies define that relationship in terms of the employee contribution to business processes. By enhancing employee motivation and skills, the efficiency and flexibility of such processes is increased, thereby leading to better business performance. What is distinctive about the human capital perspective, however, is that it defines the link between employment and business performance in terms of assets, not processes.

The importance of establishing an asset link between employment policy and business strategy is that it locates HR practices firmly in the context of the resource-based theory of the firm (Grant, 1991). This theory argues that firm competitiveness comes not from the fit that managers achieve between their strategy and their market environment, but rather from the unique and inimitable capabilities that the firm generates through its own learning processes over a significant period of time (Wernerfelt, 1984). In this view, HR practices are competitively important not because they fit employees to the requirements of business processes, but because they acquire, develop and retain human capital that is not available to other firms. In this light, human capital is one of the key assets that drive value creation. Business processes are the means by which firms develop and mobilise this key asset.

The human capital perspective thus provides a new rationale for the role of the HR function. HR is no longer viewed as a cost centre, but rather as an asset provider. For example, it is argued in the accounting literature that investments in human capital cannot be capitalised because of employee rights of labour mobility. However, depending on the context, there may be important constraints on such mobility and firms may develop their own means of retaining valued employees. This applies to some extent in regulated labour markets such as football or where labour markets are very localised, or where competencies are firm specific, making transfer difficult. Where any such factors apply, investments in training and learning might usefully be viewed as investments in human capital (Amir and Livne, 2001).

The development of a human capital perspective on the organisation would clearly have important benefits for management decision-making. Such a perspective could help to:

- guide the management of the most talented or knowledge-intensive work groups

- balance short-term or cost-driven tendencies in management with recognition of the long-term benefits of training and development

- increase the firm's capacity to innovate

- facilitate the acquisition of key skills such as leadership by enabling the firm to better compete for, develop and retain talented individuals

- aid the development of mergers or corporate restructuring by enabling the systematic identification of people with the key skills to run the new organisation

- avoid the loss of key people.

Moreover, such a perspective may not only yield benefits; it may also prevent losses. For without a more robust understanding of the nature, distribution and value of their employees' human capital, firms risk losing or downgrading that which they already have. Training and development is also likely to be more scattergun if there is no systematic assessment of its contribution to key employee competencies.

Ultimately, a human capital perspective may even challenge axial assumptions about the nature of the employment relationship. Davenport (1999), for example, argues that viewing employees as assets is misleading. Firms do not own their employees and employees are not passive. Davenport argues instead that employees would better be viewed as investors of human capital – their employment choices representing their view of the firms that provide the best return on their knowledge and skills. Indeed, he goes on to argue

that firms may need to abandon their focus on the full-time employment relationship and refocus their attention on a spreading network of relationships with external human capital providers. This is an argument which has important ramifications for HR practice, and helps to underline the distinction between an HR and a human capital model of firm performance.

Finally, one other consideration is the language of human capital itself. Because managers, especially HR managers, are constantly interacting with employees, many feel uncomfortable with a perspective that seems to reduce these employees to the status of economic units. This may be one of the reasons why managers are happier to talk about 'talent' as a way of describing their employees' skills.

Researching human capital

This study is exploratory in scope. It was undertaken over a six-month period by Dr Juanita Elias of the University of Leicester and Professor Harry Scarbrough of the University of Warwick. Given the many different interpretations of human capital and the multifaceted nature of the concept, a broadly-based definition was adopted. Human capital was defined for the purposes of our study as 'the competencies which employees apply to the production of goods and services for an employer'. The study was concerned primarily with describing and analysing existing practice in this field, and the focus of the fieldwork was on leading organisations that had more developed approaches. The level of co-operation that firms were able to provide varied according to management time and other constraints. However, our final sample of 19 managers from 10 organisations included 11 director-level managers, a number of them being HR directors.

Research within each firm was focused on interviews with key respondents – that is, those managers who were identified to us as playing a leading role in the development or implementation of the company's approach to human capital. Our aim here was to gather data not only on the particular systems or measures that had been developed within the firm, but also to examine the way in which these systems had developed over a period of time – allowing us to identify the learning that had taken place amongst managers as to the useful features of a particular system. In addition, we sought as far as possible to relate the approaches adopted by our case-study firms to the organisational contexts in which they were developed, either through access to secondary sources or through interviews with managers outside the leading group.

This research method was designed to capture the experience of a wide range of firms drawn from a diverse range of sectors. Obviously, it brought with it some limitations. We were not able, given the timescale and the number of firms involved, to interview extensively across other management functions or to speak to employees about their experience of the company's approach. This clearly limited our ability to explore the wider context of each approach, or to evaluate the costs and benefits at a level of detail. Nor were we able to track the development of company approaches to human capital in real time over a significant time period – relying instead on limited retrospective data.

It is also worth noting that while this report talks about 'evaluating human capital', this was not a term that was in use in any of the organisations we studied. Indeed, there was some resistance to the concept of 'human capital' which some managers felt reduced employees to the status of economic units. These companies did possess, however, extensive systems for measuring and reporting on the knowledge and skills of their employees – systems which were linked in various ways to management practice. In reporting on their efforts here, therefore, we are viewing these systems and practices from a human capital perspective, and not focusing narrowly on the terminology employed. On the other hand, our study does provide a useful snapshot view of the range of systems, measures and practices used to evaluate human capital in a number of leading firms. As such it provides us with an important platform for further analysis and debate, giving us some valuable insights into both the opportunities and challenges facing firms that seek to develop more systematic ways of evaluating their employees' competencies.

In reviewing existing practices, the aim was not to identify the one best approach to human capital or to produce a generic formula which captured the value of the employee contribution to firm performance. Rather, we have tried to discover, analyse and relate the different ways in which leading firms are progressing their efforts to better develop and make use of their employees' competencies. The case for developing a better understanding of human capital and embedding that, through measures or systems, in management practice is well established. A number of approaches already exist, some focused on identifying competencies for development or succession planning, others on the valuation of human capital. Through the analysis of existing good practice, this report aims to propose a framework for the evaluation of human capital that can guide the development of new systems and practices in this area.

2 | Review of the existing literature

Introduction

The recognition that much of the value added created by firms is becoming more dependent upon assets other than physical capital has stimulated the development of a wide and varied literature in the area of intellectual capital and intangible assets. Much focus has been placed on the role of knowledge and information as the new 'drivers of company life' (Bontis and Dragonetti, 1999). In this context, one of the key elements of a firm's intellectual capital is seen to be its human capital. The concept of human capital rests upon an understanding of employees as assets that contribute to the value-creating capacity of the firm.

The human capital issue presents many challenges for employers. First and foremost, viewing workers as an asset undermines traditional accountancy methodologies, which tend to report human capital only in terms of the costs associated with wages and training whilst failing to recognise the contribution that people make to the value of the organisation. Such methodologies are increasingly being questioned by the dramatic difference between actual market values and the net asset values produced by historic accounting methodology (Caddy, 2000).

This conventional accounting approach to human capital effectively denies the possibility of employees being viewed as an asset of the firm. Thus, the conventional treatment of all expenditures on employees, such as salaries and training costs, is to view them as current expenses. This is embodied in international accounting standards which define what can be regarded as an intangible asset in the following terms:

An intangible asset should be recognized if, and only if: (a) it is probable that the future economic benefits that are attributable to the asset will flow to the enterprise; and (b) the cost of the asset can be measured reliably. International Accounting Standard No. 38 (IASC 1998, parag. 19)

In short, there are several hurdles to be cleared before the cost of acquiring and developing human capital can be strictly defined as an asset. First, an asset must possess a potential for future benefits. Second, benefits must be measured in monetary terms. And third, these future benefits, which might include a contribution to future net cash flows, or cost savings, must be owned or controlled by the firm (Flamholtz, 1999). But while the human capital concept challenges conventional accounting criteria, it also raises questions concerning how employees should be managed in order to enhance the contribution of their human capital to the success of the organisation.

The following review of the human capital literature aims to address these issues and to review some of the problems that have been raised concerning the concept of human capital. The review is structured as follows: first, the concept of human capital is introduced and the debates regarding human capital are placed within the broader context of debates regarding the evolution of the so-called 'new economy' or 'knowledge economy'. Second, the focus shifts to an examination of the available approaches to the reporting and measurement of human capital and the problems that have been identified in generating robust metrics. Finally, we conclude by reviewing issues of human capital management, focusing on areas such as the recruitment and retention of talented staff.

The emergence of the concept

The term 'human capital' first appeared in 1961 in an *American Economic Review* paper by Theodore Schultz. In the 1960s and 1970s, the first wave of economic theory on human capital sought to analyse the relationship between education and economic indicators. In particular, the initial studies established a strong correlation between educational attainment and future income. This correlation is still evident today. It provides support for the view that the development of skills, knowledge and experience is associated with economic growth and increases in productivity. But while these initial studies established a broad correlation between education and economic indicators at the macro level, the causalities involved remained uncertain. Subsequent studies suggested that the role of education might lie more in the awarding of credentials and socialisation than in the development of knowledge. The correlation between education and income was found to be more non-linear, segmented and qualitatively discontinuous than human capital theory initially suggested (OECD, 1996).

The level of analysis of the early studies of human capital was macro-economic. Indeed, this is still a major strand in the economics literature, much of it focusing on the link between human capital and economic growth in under-developed countries. However, since that early period, a number of studies have sought to apply the human capital concept to the level of the firm. Writing in the 1970s, for example, Culyer and Wiseman commented that the human capital literature was well developed in the areas of education and training, health and income distribution. However, they argued that the concept also needed to be understood within the specific institutional conditions of the business organisation (Culyer and Wiseman, 1977:17).

This firm-level focus has been advanced through many different studies, with Gary Becker's (1975) work especially influential. This applies a concept of human capital that is similar to theories of physical capital. In human capital theory, reference is made to people and skills, whilst in theories of physical capital, reference is made to plant and equipment. A theory of human capital places emphasis on the way in which employee competencies create value for the organisation in the same way that the ownership of physical capital (this might be something like an oil field or a factory building) contributes to the performance of the firm. Thus, applying human capital theory to view the 'worker as an asset' has significant implications for management practice. It leads to the conclusion that firms need to redefine the costs associated with remuneration, training and development and career progression as investments that create value for the business.

Viewing employees as assets also has implications for the way in which we measure the value of an organisation, in particular, measures of the value-creating capacity of an organisation's employees (Culyer and Wiseman, 1977). Human resource accounting (HRA), which emerged as a topic of study in the 1960s, sought to address the financial valuation of human assets (Hermanson, 1964). The objective of HRA is to 'quantify the economic value of people in an organisation' (Sackman *et al*, 1989: 235). This represented a profound challenge to orthodox accountancy which was unable to encompass the non-financial, more intangible and less easily measurable aspects of company value. Although we examine HRA in more detail below in the section on measurement, it is worth noting that the issues raised in this literature are remarkably close to those that have emerged in the intellectual capital literature of the 1990s (Roslender and Dyson, 1992).

Intangible assets and the knowledge economy

Most of the recent writings on human capital place their discussion within the context of debates relating to the importance of intangible assets in the 'knowledge economy' (Berkowitz, 2001; Drake, 1998; Leadbeater, 2000; Mayo, 2001; Miller and Wurzburg, 1995; Roos *et al*, 1997; Sveiby, 1997). On the one hand, the growth of services in the economy has increased the proportion of economic outputs which are intangible. At the same time, the sources of value in this kind of economy are also increasingly intangible. In a highly integrated, global economy, the competitive pressure to produce more 'knowledge-rich' products has increased. In this context one commentator has claimed that business success 'comes down to developing, orchestrating and owning intangible assets which your competitors will find hard to imitate but which your customers value' (Teece, 1998: 45).

Intangible assets are a broader category than human capital. It includes items such as copyright, R&D capacity, work systems for the shopfloor and management, brands, customer service/relations and company image. A recent OECD report (Young, 1998) classified the principal intangible investments into six core activities:

1. Computer-related investment (software, databases, etc).

2. Production & technology (R&D, design, etc).

3. Human resources (training, learning by doing, etc).

4. Organisation of the firm (new working methods, networking, etc).

5. Marketing (advertising, market research, etc).

6. A residual category of industry-specific intangibles.

Human capital is thus usually seen as one element of a sub-set of intangibles that have been labelled 'intellectual capital' – that is, assets which are based on knowledge and learning. The Arthur Andersen Next Generation Research group (GROUP, 1998) study, for example, distinguishes between four types of intellectual assets:

1. Human Capital – the ability of individuals to apply solutions to customers' needs; competencies; and mind-sets.

2. Customer Capital – the strength of the customer relationship; superior customer-perceived value, increasing customisation of solutions.

3. Organisational Capital – the capabilities of the organisation; made up of codified knowledge from all sources – knowledge bases, business processes – the shared culture, values and norms.

4. Intellectual Capital – the balance of human, customer, and organisational capital that optimises the organisation's value space, which is its ability to generate a return on assets to stakeholders.

Human capital in particular has been emphasised in writings on 'knowledge-intensive firms' where 'the firm's most valuable knowledge will reside in the brains of its key knowledge workers' (Burton-

Jones, 2001: 39). Such firms have often been presented as the models for organisations of the future (Porter-Liebeskind, 2000: 299–301). Sadler and Milmer, for example, present the example of the European Space Agency, in which the bulk of the organisation's staff are classified as 'A grade' scientists, engineers and managers, with only a minimal number of persons employed in skilled production work (Sadler and Milmer, 1993: 24). The growing importance of human capital is not confined, however, to knowledge-intensive firms. Under growing pressures to innovate and to respond to turbulent competitive environments, there is widespread recognition across all industrial sectors that the know-how, imagination and creativity of employees is becoming at least as critical to business success as 'hard' assets (Zimmerman, 2001: 32).

Reporting and measuring human capital

Having traced the emergence of the *concept* of human capital, we now turn to available methods and tools for *reporting* human capital. The aim here is, first, to consider how human capital relates to other intangible sources of value, and, second, to explore in greater detail what behaviours and characteristics make human capital such a valuable asset.

There are many tools and systems for measuring human capital currently available, in either a generic or a proprietary form. We shall not attempt to address all of the available tools and metrics, but focus on those tools and metrics that have achieved the greatest currency. The latter tend to comprise two different categories; one is a heuristic element to do with 'balancing' consideration of people factors against other aspects of organisational performance; the second element is more forensic – it seeks to

systematically quantify the human capital of individuals and/or the organisation. The latter category can itself be broken down into financially-based approaches that view human capital as having an additive and convertible value, and non-financial approaches that are based on the comparative analysis of particular dimensions of competence.

The following discussion reviews some of the approaches that have been advocated in the literature regarding the measurement of human capital. There is a vast number of different models that have emerged from both accountancy and management circles. The purpose here is not to provide an overview of all of these approaches but to select examples of the different approaches that are representative of the literature as a whole. In general it is found that there are two main approaches to the measurement of human capital. On the one hand, there are those measures that are concerned primarily with accountancy issues relating to the external reporting of a firm's intangible assets (including human capital). On the other hand, there are those measurement systems that are used in order to generate data that are useful for internal reporting and may even feed into the strategic management of the organisation.

External reporting

The emerging consensus that in a knowledge-based economy people are an organisation's greatest asset has created an opportunity for further development of accounting approaches to human capital (Roslender and Dyson, 1992). Given that there is an increasing divergence between the book and market value of a firm in knowledge-intensive sectors, it is no surprise that concerns have re-emerged regarding the inadequacy of traditional accounting methods (Bassi *et al*, 2000: 336; Sveiby, 1997: 3).

Many of the approaches to human capital evaluation found in the literature situate the process of measuring the value of human assets alongside other intangible assets (Bontis and Dragonetti, 1999; Fincham and Roslender, 2001). Often these approaches have emerged from accountancy circles and are part of a broader approach toward the measurement of a firm's intellectual capital. This approach to evaluating human capital is thus broadly in line with that which has been pursued by the Skandia group, who view the evaluation of human capital as taking place alongside the measurement and reporting of intellectual capital.

HRA in particular reflects the concern that there is a need to account not only for 'hard' financial metrics but also for 'soft' or people-related assets that create value and drive performance in organisations. However, critics of the HRA model have pointed out that it rests upon a large number of assumptions concerning the people working within an organisation. In a typical HRA calculation, the size of the workforce is multiplied by the average unit salary costs, which is then multiplied by an estimate of the average length of tenure per employee and an estimate of the average increase in wages per year, and then discounted back to year one. Although the resulting figure is purported to represent a unit of human capital value, the level of subjectivity and uncertainty means that the figures lack the reliability that is required to meaningfully account for the value of human assets (Bontis and Dragonetti, 1999). Furthermore, the usefulness of a figure that represents the human capital value of a firm largely in terms of future wage increases and length of tenure is open to question. It may

tell us little about the valuable skills and accumulated knowledge of key talented individuals at a firm. A further problem with the HRA approach is that it overlooks many of the softer skills and competencies associated with human capital. In other words, it neglects the 'competence', 'attitude' and 'intellectual ability' (Roos *et al*, 1997) that can be viewed as constituting human capital.

HRA thus represents an approach that in many ways provides only a very general picture concerning a firm's human assets. Such general figures may, however, be useful for external reporting purposes, enabling firms to report the kinds of data that would enable investors to make better informed judgements about the way in which firms are best utilising their human assets. Many such approaches place the measurement of human capital within the context of other intangible assets and focus on external reporting, with many writers making the case for putting human capital on the balance sheet (Berkowitz, 2001).

The challenge facing companies, however, is to go beyond strictly financial measures and identify and report on the dynamics and value within that company. There may be little point in providing more information on all intangibles *per se*. Stakeholders are likely to be interested only in those intangibles that will drive future value.

Yet despite these calls for greater transparency, Bassi *et al* (Bassi, Baruch, Low, McMurrer and Siesfeld, 2000) find that few firms actually disclose non-financial information. Where annual reports do contain information relevant to the firm's human capital, this is usually qualitative information and of such a general nature to be of little value for any deeper analysis. Furthermore, other studies note an actual decline in the number of companies actually reporting human capital information (Westphalen, 1999).

One measure of human capital that has enjoyed widespread legitimacy in the eyes of the financial community is Economic Value Added (EVA). Of those measurement systems that view human capital alongside intellectual capital, EVA is one of the most well known. Developed by the New York consultancy Stern Stewart & Co, EVA is a holistic approach to financial management that attempts to tie together capital budgeting, financial planning, goal setting, performance measurement, shareholder communication and incentive compensation (Bontis and Dragonetti, 1999). The objective of EVA is to establish a common language amongst managers and investors concerning how value is created, with the express purpose of maximising shareholder value. Young (Young, 1998; Young and O'Byrne, 2001) suggests that EVA is useful in that it creates a shared understanding of value creation and leads to appropriate metrics that management can draw upon and use to compare different projects. However, the EVA approach has been criticised because of its continued reliance upon cost-based accountancy methods.

EVA has been applied to human resource management in the work of Fitz-Enz and the Saratoga Institute (Fitz-Enz, 2000). Using the EVA framework, this approach involves deriving metrics from the key drivers of value for the organisation. This approach reflects a commitment to having robust metrics that can actually tell us how future performance can be derived from successful HR systems. These metrics fall into three groups:

- ◘ *The overall enterprise – how human capital contributes to the value-creating capacity of the organisation; the most commonly used metric is 'revenue per employee'. This is calculated by dividing company revenues by the number of full-time equivalent employees.*

- ◘ *Processes and function that enhance service, quality and productivity. Here metrics encompass the employee contribution to critical outputs of different types of organisational activity.*

- ◘ *How the human capital itself is managed. The relevant metrics here address the effectiveness of HR activities within the firm.*

(Mayo, 2001)

As Mayo notes, in relation to the enterprise as a whole,

Yet despite the tying of the Saratoga approach to an EVA method, the focus on specifically HR issues means that the development of metrics is designed more for internal managerial functions than for external reporting to potential investors.

Indeed, HR-specific indices are different from external accounting because they are less about the reporting of human assets, and more concerned with finding the best ways to manage these assets. The discussion below, therefore, turns to examining the way in which techniques for the internal reporting of human assets have been addressed in the literature on human capital.

Internal reporting
Human capital and identifying sources of value

Identifying sources of value or 'performance drivers' is an essential element in the evaluation of human capital. Firms need to have a clear idea of their greatest sources of value to be able to make appropriate investments in human capital (LeBlanc, Mulvey and Rich, 2000). By linking good HR practice and strategic management to human capital measurement, firms are able to make a number of better-informed decisions that will help to ensure long-term business success.

This aim is something that has been addressed by the consultancy firm Watson Wyatt through the construction of a human capital index – a survey of companies that has linked together HR management practices and market value. Their findings suggested that four major categories of HR practice could be linked to a 30 per cent increase in shareholder value creation, as illustrated in Table 2.1, below. First, a commitment to recruiting excellence – hiring the right people and developing recruitment practices that support the strategic aims of the business. Second, clear rewards and accountability, including such practices as the distribution of share options more widely to employees, and career systems that act to reward to high achievers and either terminate the employment of poor performers or offer them coaching for improvement. Third, they stress the importance of a collegial and flexible workplace in which flexible work arrangements are accompanied by the encouragement of teamwork

and co-operation and a focus on employee satisfaction. Finally, these firms are shown to have a high level of integrity in their communications, with transparent and accountable business practices and clearly stated corporate goals and objectives.

What the human capital index does, therefore, is to make linkages between individual employee performance (or competence) and the wider issue of corporate culture. This is also something that is stressed by Zwell and Ressler (Zwell and Ressler, 2000) who suggest that although the best way to measure human capital is to focus on competencies, any assessment of employee performance cannot be done in isolation from an honest examination of the firm's strengths and weaknesses overall.

Importantly, the Watson Wyatt consultancy discovered that certain HR initiatives will not create value for the organisation – and this is especially the case when the HR initiative was not directly supporting the objectives of the organisation. Such findings thus underline the case for having systems in place for the evaluation of human capital that focus on the effectiveness of different HR practices in developing a firm's human capital base.

The human capital index shares certain similarities with a number of other approaches to human capital measurement that have sought to create indices of best practice. Similar approaches are found, for example, in William Mercer's Human Capital Wheel, The European Business Excellence Model, and the Malcolm Baldridge criteria for performance excellence, and Arthur Andersen's Fit-Cost-Value framework (Mayo, 2001: 47–53). However, there are also important differences in nuance between these approaches. The human capital index, for instance, does not have the bespoke features of the Mercer wheel, which is tailored to individual organisations.

Table 2 | Impact of human capital

Human capital dimension	Expected change in market value (per cent)
Recruitment excellence	10.1
Clear rewards and accountability	9.2
Collegial, flexible workplace	7.8
Communications integrity	4.0

Balanced scorecard

One of the most well-known techniques that aligns the evaluation of human capital to the company's strategic aims is the balanced scorecard (Kaplan and Norton, 1996). This approach was developed to counter the tendency to focus too narrowly on financial objectives in the development of strategy. The scorecard has four elements: financial (eg cash flow and return on capital employed) measures of innovation; customer (eg market share, customer retention and loyalty, and customer profitability); internal business process (eg cycle times, quality and productivity); and learning and innovation (eg percentage of revenues from new products, R&D success rate). The model as a whole represents multiple objectives and provides targets that have to be accomplished. In this way the scorecard provides a control mechanism within an organisation rather than simply the basis for periodic reporting. The scorecard is aimed at helping executives measure the effectiveness of their business strategy in delivering financial results. It is widely used in the USA and it has also been adopted in the UK, especially by firms in the financial services sector.

The balanced scorecard advocates the development of measures that meet the needs of businesses and that vary over time. For example, within the learning and innovation theme, there are a number of measures of human capital, including employee satisfaction, employee retention and productivity, and the extent of human resource staffing gaps.

Through the device of the balanced scorecard, a firm's human capital investments can be linked to other business performance measures – something that was identified as important in the Watson

Wyatt Human Capital Index. The balanced scorecard approach is about setting objectives and how well these objectives are being met. These objectives are as follows:

- *Financial* – to succeed financially, how should we appear to shareholders?

- *Customer* – to achieve our vision, how should we appear to customers?

- *Internal business process* – to satisfy our shareholders and customers, at what business process must we excel?

- *Learning and growth* – to achieve our vision, how shall we sustain our ability to change and improve?

These objectives concern the need to transform strategy into objectives and are accompanied by targets that must be met in each area. In many ways the balanced scorecard approach is rather non-specific about how human capital should be measured. The significant impact of this approach, however, is to incorporate different perspectives on firm performance in the process of target setting. Thus, it combines elements of intangible assets and human capital with more traditional financial metrics in the way that it views the company. At the same time, this approach places a focus on both long- and short-terms goals (Norton, 2001). Finally, it is a device that can be used and understood by all stakeholders in the organisation – unlike financial statements, which are targeted at shareholders.

Olve et al (Olve et al, 1999) note that, given the very simplicity of the basic concept of the balanced scorecard, the concept has been adapted within different organisations to suit their business needs.

The aim of the balanced scorecard is in many ways to develop measures that meet the needs of the business over time, with firms encouraged to include 4–7 different measures within each of the perspectives on the scorecard (up to a total of 25 different metrics). These measures will, of course, be designed with the specific needs of the particular organisation in mind. In this sense, the balanced scorecard is a useful device for giving some kind of measurement of how the firm is performing against a range of self-defined standards that are both financial and non-financial. However, it is not capable of producing rigorous universal metrics for the measurement and evaluation of human capital.

HR scorecard

The balanced scorecard approach is endorsed by writers such as Brian E. Becker, Mark A. Huselid and Dave Ulrich, whose book, *The HR Scorecard*, makes the case for HR-based measurement systems to be clearly linked to the firm's strategic aims and values (Becker *et al*, 2001). Their view is based on a model of firm performance which identifies a critical role for the HR function and HR systems. This role, which they term 'HR's strategic architecture', identifies a strong causal relationship between the HR function (HR professionals with strategic competencies), the HR system (high performance, strategically aligned policies and practices) and employee behaviours (strategically focused competencies, motivations and associated behaviours). In short, their concern is with the impact of HR activities on the human capital of the firm. In this context, the aim of developing an HR scorecard was to move from the general finding that effective HR management systems can contribute to business success, to ensuring that they actually do contribute to success in a particular firm. To do so, they suggest, firms must implement a strategic HR measurement system,

the 'HR scorecard' – 'a measurement system that convincingly showcases HR's impact on business performance' (p.4). They point out that although human capital measurement systems are designed to identify the sources or drivers of value, a more important factor is management's ability to demonstrate the importance of such measures. They claim, for instance, that 'at Sears, a mere 4 per cent increase in employee satisfaction reverberated through the profit chain, eventually lifting market capitalisation by nearly $250 million' (p.15). It is in this sense that their work follows the balanced scorecard model, because creating an HR scorecard rests upon the idea that the employees of a firm see the connection between their everyday work and the firm's strategic objectives. Measurement systems are an important component of the HR scorecard because they provide essential information concerning how well the firm is meeting its strategic objectives. However, Becker *et al* do not detail a specific system for the measurement of human capital. They argue that this is something that should be designed in relation to the firm's strategic objectives.

The HR scorecard builds upon approaches such as the human capital index that have sought to identify how HR systems can drive the value-creating capacity of organisations. Although models such as the human capital index underline the need for HR initiatives to be monitored and evaluated in terms of corporate goals and strategic objectives, the HR scorecard makes the case for the measurement of the effectiveness of human resource practices and policies in terms of the firm's human capital. In other words, the HR scorecard poses the question: is this initiative allowing my business to achieve its strategic aims through the most effective use of its human capital assets?

However, the scorecard approach is not beyond criticism. Mayo identifies a problem with these techniques; namely, that although they are widely used within organisations as a form of performance measurement, they are not generally linked to data concerning the value of people within an organisation. Mayo comments that what is needed is a connected framework that relates the asset value of people to their contribution and takes account of conditions that maximise contribution (Mayo, 2002). In a sense, Mayo is arguing for more robust metrics to be incorporated into these human capital evaluation systems. There is, he argues, a need for data concerning both the 'human asset worth' of an organisation and at the same time an assessment of the worth of individual competencies (through the construction of an 'individual asset multiplier'). Such calls for more rigorous, and possibly even standardised, metrics are often justified on the grounds that 'what gets measured gets managed' (Murphy and Zandvakili, 2000).

Andrew Mayo

As noted above, one of the most recent contributions to the human capital debate comes from Andrew Mayo. Seeking to build on McGregor's seminal text, 'The human side of enterprise', Mayo seeks to identify the 'human value of the enterprise'. His major thesis is that there is a 'lack of balance between thinking of people as costs and viewing them as assets' (Mayo, 2001: 4). He then outlines several challenges to achieving this balance:

1. Balance cost numbers with value numbers so that both have equal status in decision-making.

2. How do we recognise the intrinsic diversity in the worth of people and find a way to value it through understanding their personal human capital?

3. We need to measure the value – financial and non-financial – that is added to each stakeholder by each individual in our organisation.

4. We must be able to value future returns from intangible and people-related investments with as much credibility as the well-tried methodologies for physical asset investment.

5. It is as important to measure the drivers of performance as it is to measure the outcomes themselves.

6. How do we ensure that value is increased and not lost when organisations merge and restructure?

7. We need to know how to obtain relevant and reliable data on intangible assets within the organisation before we are required to publish it externally.

To address these challenges, Mayo advocates the use of a 'human capital monitor', this includes a formula for calculating the 'human asset worth' of individual employees. Thus, 'human asset worth' is defined as equal to 'employment cost x individual asset multiplier/1000'. The individual asset multiplier is defined as a weighted average assessment of capability, potential, contribution to stakeholder value, and alignment to organisational values.

This understanding of human capital is very similar to that proposed by David Ulrich who suggested that human capital consisted of a multiplication of employee competence and employee commitment (Ulrich, 1998: 15–26).

Skandia Navigator

The Skandia company has long utilised elements of the balanced scorecard in its approach to the measurement of intellectual capital. In the case of Skandia, experimentation with intellectual capital reporting dates back to the mid-1990s (Edvinsson and Malone,1997). Thus, Skandia's 'balanced' annual reports contain non-financial supplements in which a small number of strategic indicators provide information on the success of efforts to grow the intellectual capital of business units.

These range from widely utilised examples such as profit margin and value added per employee, to more progressive ones such as the number of women leaders and the percentage of employees working from home.

The Skandia Navigator (Figure 2) is a collection of critical measurements that aim to provide a more balanced view of performance and goal achievement. Five perspectives capture different areas of interest, each one of them visualising the value creation process. The Navigator thus combines historical financial accounting (historical measures of company performance) with measures designed to examine the current position of the firm (customer focus) as well as future success (a development focus). Within each 'focus' of the Navigator, rather like the 'perspectives' in the

Figure 2 | The Skandia Navigator

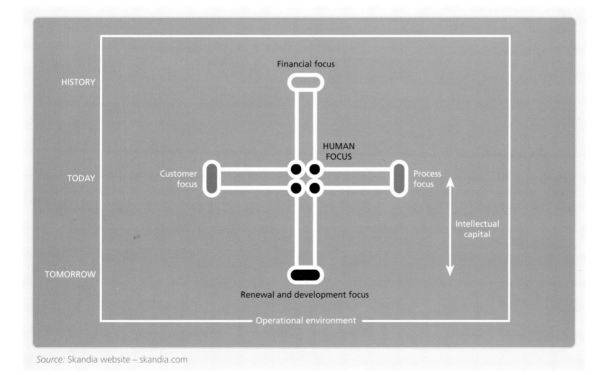

Source: Skandia website – skandia.com

balanced scorecard, are a small number of strategic indicators which aim to generate information concerning the success of attempts to develop the intellectual capital of the business units of the firm. Earlier, it was noted that the Skandia model views human capital as a fundamental component in the intellectual capital of the firm and it would seem that the focus concerned with renewal and development (the future) is most relevant to this area. Such measures in this focus have included things such as value added per employee as well as the number of persons identified as leaders, and even the proportion of these leaders who are women. There was considerable flexibility in the use of these indicators, with different business units of the Skandia group working to develop their own specific Navigators (Roy, 1999), whilst personal Navigators were also put forward as a means through which the company could track the performance of individual employees.

Skandia themselves describe the Navigator in the following terms:

To make sure that we are working towards our vision and strategic objectives and they will come true through our daily work, we need to visualize and translate them into concrete and measurable activities. We need a structure to help us learn from each other and make sure that our daily efforts do contribute to Skandia's overall strategic objectives. But the most important aspect of this work is how to communicate the vision and the strategic objectives to the organization as a whole. The Skandia Navigator is our tool for implementing the overall vision and strategic objectives all through the organization. (www.skandia.com)

A key issue for Skandia was to ascertain how far the value of the company derived from non-financial assets. Thus, the firm recognised the need to gain an understanding of the drivers of

Figure 3 | The Skandia Value Scheme

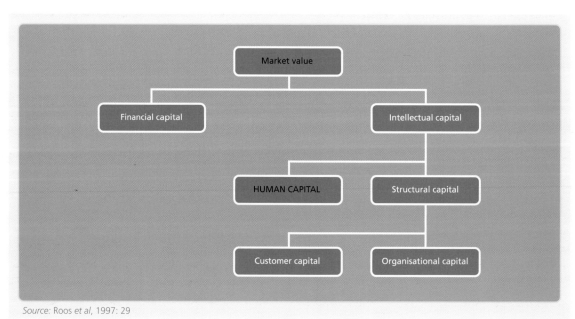

Source: Roos *et al*, 1997: 29

company performance, especially given that many intangible assets (including human capital) are different from physical capital in that they can appreciate in value and are in this sense crucial to future business success (LeBlanc *et al*, 2000). In the 'Skandia Value Scheme' human capital is viewed as a component part of the intellectual capital of an organisation (Figure 3).

This model is a useful starting-point in conceptualising human capital as part of the wider 'intellectual capital' of an organisation. As can be seen from Figure 3, the firm views market value as stemming from both financial capital (ie those company assets that are traditionally recorded on company balance sheets) and intellectual capital. Intellectual capital itself is subdivided into human capital (the parts of an organisation that think) and structural capital (defined as what is left when the people go home). This structural capital is then subdivided into customer capital and organisational capital (in other words, looking at how intellectual capital is derived from both external and internal processes and practices). Within the firm, the organisational capital is divided into innovation and process capital. Process capital represents the way in which know-how is captured through, for example, training manuals or intranet systems, whilst innovation capital is viewed as 'what creates the success of tomorrow' (Roos *et al*, 1997: 29).

Although individuals may leave the firm at the end of the day, the team-based competencies, work-systems and intellectual property that they have helped to create remain rooted within the organisation. Human capital may have played a role in the formation of these forms of capital – but they are effectively 'owned' by and stay with the organisation. By contrast, human capital can never truly be owned by the organisation: people

are able to move to other organisations and thereby take their human capital with them – thus raising problems with the extent to which human capital can ever really be regarded as an 'asset'.

Roos *et al* (1997) have proposed a further subdivision of the human capital category included in the Skandia model. Human capital, for these authors, is comprised of 'competence', 'attitude' and 'intellectual ability', or what they term different 'human abilities'. The word 'competence' is used to refer to the knowledge that individual workers have, including both the skills and qualifications that they had before joining the workforce and those that they have acquired since they began working for the firm. 'Attitude' refers to the motivation, behaviour and conduct of individuals, whilst 'intellectual agility' relates to the ability of employees to apply the knowledge that they have to the workplace environment.

Competence systems

Many of the methods and tools outlined above seek to review the human capital of the organisation as a whole – to provide aggregate indicators of the development of human capital which can be used to balance financial indicators. The bedrock of human capital evaluation, however, can be regarded as the organisation's ability to evaluate the human capital of individual employees. Without an understanding of the nature of key skills and their relevance to particular contexts, it is questionable whether broader aggregate data can be properly validated.

For this reason, the centrepiece of many of our case firms' efforts to evaluate human capital was their systems for classifying and evaluating the competence of their employees. Such systems were often developed for a variety of different

> "...the idea of evaluating employee competence can be traced back historically to Taylor's principles of scientific management."

reasons, as outlined below. They were certainly not developed simply with a focus on the evaluation of human capital. Indeed, we need to acknowledge that the notion of competence has evolved over a significant time period. Thus, the idea of evaluating employee competence can be traced back historically to Taylor's principles of scientific management. In its modern usage, however, the term developed in the HRM literature of the 1970s and 1980s (Boyatzis, 1982). It is broadly defined as the relationship between employees and work tasks. The parameters of competence are thus defined not simply by the employee's knowledge and skills – not all of these may be relevant to task performance. Rather, competence is made up of knowledge and skills which are required to perform a specific task effectively (McClelland). It is defined as 'an underlying characteristic of an individual that is causally related to … superior performance in a job or situation' (Spencer and Spencer, 1993: 9).

In the 1980s and 1990s, this view of competence was advanced on two fronts. First, one group of scholars has claimed that changes in the nature of work are making job-based definitions of competence increasingly irrelevant. The idea of being able to specify work demands in terms of a particular job description and then selecting for that description seems increasingly anachronistic in an era of flexible, knowledge-based organisations. Thus, Lawler and Ledford (1992) claim that job-based approaches to competence are designed for mass production, but are inappropriate for an era in which the competence and motivation of individuals are key resources. They argue that competencies should be focused on the individual, and not the job. A second criticism of conventional approaches to competence comes from Sandberg (1994) who argues that such approaches put too

much emphasis on the managerial attempt to produce an objective listing of employee attributes. This, he argues, neglects the importance of the employees' own perception of their work.

Developments in the classification and measurement of employee competencies are driven by a number of different business needs. Some of these help to provide a link between human capital and strategy, for example by highlighting skills gaps in different parts of the organisation. Others relate to determining the training and development needs of individuals. Rosenbaum, for instance, points out that in many organisations managers have insufficient information about employees' abilities and are therefore forced to rely on other signals, in particular previous attainments, in deciding how much training and development to provide for a particular individual (Rosenbaum, 1984). Again, where competencies are linked to the company appraisal system they may help to provide a basis not only for development but also for reward. Finally, there are business pressures toward the better allocation of human capital internally – specifically, the need to allocate individuals to projects based on their competencies.

More recently, the development of IT systems coupled with the advent of knowledge management has encouraged attempts to develop IT-based competence systems. These range from relatively simple forms, such as 'expert directories' listing employees' areas of expertise, to more sophisticated databases that seek to represent the scope and depth of employee competencies in a systematic way. Although such competence systems could arguably be used to highlight the organisation's skills base to external groups, such as would-be customers, they are typically employed for internal HRM purposes only. In this guise, such systems have been criticised on a number of counts, including limited effectiveness, outdated information, static competence descriptions, and a lack of commitment amongst employees (Lindgren, 2002).

Despite these problems of measuring and representing competencies, there remains considerable value in the human capital perspective. Fundamentally, it raises questions about how employee competencies build value and as such challenges the short-termist financial bias that underpins much management thinking. In other words, 'there are good arguments for treating employees as if they were assets…. The principal one is that the cost of hiring, training and developing good staff is an investment in the future' (Lester, 1996: 54). This view thus has implications for HR policy and practice which extend some way beyond the temptation to use the language of human capital as another HR buzzword. We now turn, therefore, to examine the specific dilemmas that HR practitioners face in the management of human capital.

The management of human capital

It has been suggested that human capital theory is an economic tool that 'will allow managers to make a variety of better reasoned personnel decisions' (Lazear, 1998: 133). It was shown earlier, for example, that techniques such as the human capital index enable managers to identify those HR initiatives that create most value for the business. Zwell and Ressler (2000), for example, have suggested that systems of human capital measurement are the key to creating a strategic plan for HR, one that aligns people management

policies and practices with an organisation's strategic goals. Thus, areas such as recruitment, remuneration systems, training and development, or the development of career systems, can be devised so as to help contribute to the firm's human capital asset base. This is what Becker *et al* emphasise when they claim that 'for HR to create value, a firm needs to structure each element of its HR system in a way that relentlessly emphasises, supports, and reinforces a high performance work-force' (Becker *et al*, 2001: 13). But despite the perceived advantages of systems to codify and quantify human capital, their application to management practice is constrained by at least four major problems which limit their value as tools for decision-making – the problems of reductionism, attribution, ownership and valuation.

1. The reductionism problem

Existing methods of classifying and measuring human capital tend to adopt a *reductionist* approach. That is, they seek to determine its scope by distinguishing human capital from other aspects of organisational activity (Fincham and Roslender, 2001). Human capital is distinguished from structural capital, for example. The limitations of this approach are that it imposes a static set of distinctions on activities which are dynamic and interdependent. Carpenter *et al* (2001), for instance, claim that all intangible assets are embedded in human capital; in this sense human capital plays a key role in the emergence of all intellectual capital-based intangibles. Furthermore, they suggest that there are problems in viewing human capital in isolation from other sources of value, claiming that human capital works to create most value when it is 'bundled' with other tangible and intangible sources of value.

2. The attribution problem

As discussed earlier, human capital is context dependent. That is, it is defined by the relationship between the individual's knowledge and skills and the particular context in which they are being applied. Most methods for identifying and measuring human capital, however, tend to attribute human capital to the individual alone, neglecting the context. Competence systems may exacerbate this problem by implying that specific skills are universally relevant and independent of the different organisational contexts in which they might be applied. The danger is that such systems will be insufficiently sensitive to the dynamic nature of human capital – neglecting not only changes in the individual's skills that come about through learning, but also changes in context resulting from strategic shifts or restructuring.

3. The ownership problem

Given the problems associated with viewing human capital as an asset, it is interesting to note that one of the key proponents of the human capital approach has suggested that human capital should not be conceptualised as an asset of the firm at all (Davenport, 1999). Although Davenport concedes that the asset metaphor is a more useful conceptualisation of an employee's value compared to cost (pp.4–5), he suggests that it is more fruitful for firms to see their employees as investors. They are in a sense investing both in their own training and development and also in the company itself. Davenport argues that the notion of an asset implies ownership, something that cannot be claimed in terms of a firm's employees: they are free to move to another firm and, therefore, take their human capital with them. Second, Davenport suggests that assets are passive (ie 'bought, sold and replaced at the whim of their owners') whereas employees take personal responsibility for investments in their own human capital.

4. The valuation problem

Even measurement systems that do not place a financial value on competencies involve some assessment of the value of such competencies to the organisation. However, such evaluations are often undermined by a tension between the different principles of valuation that might be applied to human capital. Such capital can be viewed as having both an exchange value and a use value. The first represents the market price, the salary level, that individuals can command for their skills from potential employers. The second represents the usefulness of those skills – their ability to generate value in a particular context for a particular employer. For some skills – footballing skills, for example – competitive markets operate and the individual's value is defined primarily in terms of exchange value. In these instances, there is little need to develop systems of measurement – the market price incorporates all relevant information about the person's skills. For many other skills, however, efficient markets may not operate and there may be a significant disparity between the usefulness of an individual's skills to an employer and what he or she could command from the market. This applies particularly to more firm-specific skills. In these instances, measurement systems may be developed to identify the use value of such skills. However, given labour mobility and market uncertainty, problems may arise where exchange value clashes with the use value incorporated in the measurement system. Individuals may be more inclined to pursue skills that offer higher exchange value than those skills that are deemed to be useful to the firm.

Despite these possible problems in the evaluation of human capital, the implication of developing a human capital perspective on the sources of economic value means that HR policies and practices become viewed as crucial to business success. This is what Nordhaug (1993) has called the shift away from production-centred businesses to learning-centred businesses. In these organisations we need to address the way in which firms manage (that is, plan, acquire, develop and utilise) these competencies. Thus HR comes to take on the role of a key strategic partner in the business.

The war for talent

As we saw above, a human capital measurement system, especially one that is designed for internal reporting purposes, should enable employers to identify those competencies and abilities that drive business performance (Becker *et al*, 2001). But what are the potential impacts of such systems? One impact might be that if companies are increasingly effective at identifying the competencies that will drive their business forward, then certain individuals will be highly sought after by firms. Much of the literature on human capital suggests that there is a reliance on the skills and abilities of key talented individuals, who are usually perceived as either technical specialists or young managers of high potential. This reliance has led to claims that a 'war for talent' is enabling certain individuals to claim higher and higher salaries since firms regard the retention of these key staff as essential to business success (Hacker, 2001; Michaels *et al*, 2001). This is particularly the case in sectors that are reliant upon the skills of key individuals who are valuable to the firm in terms of their ability to generate high levels of income for their employers, or to develop innovative products or business practices

that can contribute to competitive advantage. One business analyst has thus commented that these are the people who can 'make or break an organisation' (Annunzio, 2001: 64).

The need for the effective management of talent is emphasised, in particular, in areas such as employee recruitment and retention. Nordhaug, for example, writes of recruitment as 'competence acquisition'. In human capital terms, therefore, the recruitment of key individuals who will contribute significantly to the value-creating capacity of the firm is crucial to business success. Thus, attempts to attract or headhunt employees from rival firms in other sectors are a hallmark of the war for talent. Within this competitive climate, it could be suggested, firms will find it increasingly difficult to retain key staff. Practices aimed at retaining key persons include incentives based upon pay and remuneration. The concept of the 'gold-collared worker', for example, presents a picture of talented individuals who can demand increasingly large salaries and bonuses in an economic environment in which their specific talents are in short supply. However, what also remains important is the firm's reputation as an employer in terms of opportunities for professional and personal development (Nordhaug, 1993: 30). In certain respects this desire to market oneself as a good employer explains the limited external reporting of human capital issues by firms.

However, the war for talent idea has itself been criticised. O'Reilly and Pfeffer (2000), for instance, claim that such strategies are ultimately self-defeating, since a reliance on the recruitment of highly talented individuals can be at the expense of systems designed to train and develop a firm's staff as a whole. In another paper, Pfeffer (2001) suggests that the war for talent is the 'wrong metaphor' because it overlooks the extent to

> **"It seems that companies which adopt a 'talent war' mindset may place too much value on outsiders and downplay the talent already inside the company."**

which teams of people will often operate more effectively than mere collections of individuals. It is suggested that companies need to take an approach toward the management of their workforce that emphasises the ability of all to succeed (and thereby 'achieve extraordinary results with ordinary people') (O'Reilly and Pfeffer, 2000), rather than merely emphasising the importance of the few key players. It seems that companies which adopt a 'talent war' mindset may place too much value on outsiders and downplay the talent already inside the company. They may create competitive, zero-sum dynamics that make internal learning and knowledge transfer difficult. This in turn may produce a self-fulfilling prophecy and create an attitude of arrogance instead of an attitude of wisdom (Pfeffer, 2001: 2).

For Pfeffer, organisational culture and effective people management are fundamental to developing a firm's human capital base. Nordhaug (1993) confirms this argument, suggesting that whereas general skills and knowledge can be sold in external labour markets, firm-specific competencies are valuable in one firm only. Furthermore, once generated, the marginal cost of utilising firm-specific competence is considered to be small relative to the cost of forming it through training and development. Consequently, both the firm and the employees possessing the specific knowledge and skills will normally be interested in, and benefit from, an enduring contractual employment relationship (Nordhaug, 1993: 228–9). Furthermore, an effective human capital evaluation system could enable companies to identify those individuals within the firm who are vital to business success. Indeed, the case studies presented in this report demonstrate the way in which metrics relating to employee performance

and competencies have become essential to management development and succession planning.

Training and development

The idea of a war for talent also comes into play in discussions of training and development policies within firms. As mentioned earlier, one of the problems with the concept of human capital is that companies can never be said to own their human capital in the way that they posses physical and even structural assets. This leads to a problem: 'As training becomes an ever larger investment, and less firm specific, the risk for firm owners is that they will be investing, in effect, in a public good' (Burton-Jones, 2001: 39).

Such claims would be countered, however, by Pfeffer and O'Reilly, who would claim that what really matters is employee commitment to the firm. Here, training and development programmes can play a significant role in gaining the trust of employees that the firm is investing in their future. Many skills and abilities are developed in-house within organisational cultures that are based upon trust and promote employee learning and development (Gratton, 1997). Others have emphasised the need for firms to be flexible in their employment arrangements, perhaps allowing people to leave for a while and return, or maintaining relationships with these people as consultants. But whatever a firm's level of investment in training and development, in human capital terms what is most important is that investment is targeted in order to enhance future performance. Of course, calculating the return on investment (ROI) from training programmes is a very difficult business, but devices such as the balanced scorecard do enable employers to constantly relate training and development to overall corporate objectives (Becker *et al*, 2001).

Another potential downside of the war for talent concept is that the concern with talent is at the expense of those workers employed in lower-skilled work. The rise of subcontracting and 'flexible' employment in low-skill sectors can be understood in terms of the creation of core and peripheral workforces (Atkinson, 1984). Some writers have argued, therefore, that the state needs to play a more proactive role in raising the skills and talents of the general population so that they might not be marginalised by the shift toward more knowledge-based work in the new economy (Streeck, 1989).

Others have argued that new employment relations are emerging in which it is increasingly difficult to see how the concern with human capital will translate into practice for the bulk of employees. For example, Blair and Kochan pose the following question:

Are the new employment relations and organizational forms that are emerging able to harness the ideas and skills of the people who are actually doing the work as well as or better than the old forms? (Blair and Kochan, 2000: 2)

The issue of organisational downsizing is of particular relevance to the issue of human capital management. Some have suggested, for instance, that the downsizing initiatives of the 1980s and 1990s led to a loss of organisational knowledge that has significantly hampered business success (Oates, 1992).

At the same time, it has been suggested that certain aspects of present-day corporations make it much easier for firms to enhance the skills and abilities of their workforce, and therefore build human capital. Writers such as Appelbaum and Berg (2000) have stressed, for example, the way in which new technologies enable even very large firms to engage employees in decision-making because technological changes are meaning that more and more front-line workers take on more responsible roles. In the same respect, it has also been suggested that the adoption of knowledge management technologies makes firms less reliant on the knowledge of middle managers (Oates, 1992). New technologies such as computer software programs are also making it much easier for firms to evaluate their human capital and to make HR policies more targeted and strategic.

3 | The case studies

The case-study firms

Marks & Spencer
AutoCo
Tesco
Xerox
Norwich Union Insurance (NUI)
Motorola
Shell, UK
BT
BAE Systems
CityCo

This report draws upon the experiences of a number of case-study firms. The case-study research took place over a four-month period. Firms were initially identified using Internet search engines, personal contacts and newspaper archives. Letters were sent out to firms in February and March of 2002 and the interviews were completed by the end of May 2002. As highlighted in the literature review, very little of the literature on human capital has sought to look at actual practice within UK firms (preferring to focus on abstract models and theory). The research was, therefore, exploratory in nature as we sought to avoid imposing any prescriptive conceptions on the actual practices of firms.

Given the exploratory nature of the research, the interview schedule was designed to cover a wide range of possible issues. The aim of the interviews was to establish how different firms in different sectors sought to evaluate the value-creating capacity of their workforce. In each case-study firm, we aimed to speak to a senior executive with close involvement in, and responsibility for, the evaluation of human capital. Ten firms were visited and we were able to gain access to a number of senior managers in these firms. To preserve confidentiality, we have not named the individual respondents. However, of the 19 managers who were interviewed in the course of the study, 12 were at director level, many of them being HR directors.

We have to acknowledge that none of the case study firms explicitly used the term 'human capital'. Indeed, we found some resistance to the term on the grounds that it reduced individual employees to the status of economic units. Our account of their efforts to 'evaluate human capital', then, is thus a reflection not so much of the specific terms that they employed but rather of applying the human capital perspective to their practices. Given the exploratory scope of the study, we adopted a broad operationalisation of what constituted the evaluation of human capital. Thus, any attempts to measure or assess the skills, knowledge and experience of employees were seen as relevant to the study. Applying this criterion, we found that while none of the firms would have explicitly described their practices as the evaluation of human capital, their widespread efforts to measure employee competencies amounted to exactly that.

Obviously, we need to insert a caveat here about the validity of defining practices to do with measuring competencies as functionally equivalent to the evaluation of human capital. Language is powerful. It is not just a means of representing activity, but also influences the nature of that activity – an observation that was underlined, for instance, by debates about the distinction between personnel management and HR management. Indeed, in Chapter 1, we describe the implications of a human capital perspective. The resistance of firms to the 'human capital' label certainly suggests that this 'discourse' has not been widely adopted. For our purposes, however, broad functional equivalence seemed sufficient. Thus, the

> "...in none of the firms interviewed did we see any evidence of systematic external human capital reporting..."

evaluation of human capital is effectively defined here as the measurement of employee competencies, where the measurement processes influenced the firm's employment practices in areas such as employee recruitment, retention, pay, performance appraisal, training and development, and leadership systems. Furthermore, there was recognition amongst most of the case-study firms that having systems in place for evaluating and developing human capital played a key role in creating value (be it for shareholders or customers). An emerging consensus around the value of having reliable systems in place to measure and manage employee competencies has meant that people issues are now being viewed in a much more strategic manner. Many of the case-study firms clearly recognised the importance that people strategies play in the attainment of overall company strategy. This was demonstrated, for example, by the widespread use of the balanced scorecard.

Human capital evaluation in practice, however, was characterised by the dominance of internal reporting systems over systems of external reporting. Indeed, in none of the firms interviewed did we see any evidence of systematic external human capital reporting, aside from the usual 'people statements' found in most company reports. Of our case-study firms, only Shell has argued for external reporting of human capital. This section of the report thus aims to provide a brief overview of the case-study firms, describing how human capital evaluation takes place within these organisations.

Marks & Spencer

Operating across 300 stores, Marks & Spencer is a leading UK retailer of clothing, foods, household goods and financial services, serving 10 million customers a week. There are two main elements to the way in which human capital is being evaluated at Marks & Spencer. The first is the creation of a skills map or capabilities audit that will give an accurate picture of how the firm is currently doing in terms of the skills and competencies of its employee base. The second is the work that the firm is doing in the area of employment brand and attempts to measure accurately the effects of their employment practices.

Systems and practice

At Marks & Spencer, the measurement of employee competencies is in its early stages. They are currently attempting to map their current capabilities through a skills survey that is being piloted in the Republic of Ireland. The survey seeks to identify the employees' progress in different categories of skills. First, 'portable skills' – skills that every employee should have to differing degrees – for example, IT skills. Second, 'technical skills' which relate specifically to 20 identifiable professions, or job families, within the firm. Finally, the survey also seeks to measure employee competencies in terms of sets of behaviours identified as key to organisational success. These five behaviours or 'ways of working' are outlined as follows: Think customer!; Be passionate about product; Be one team; Own your part in delivering results; Be honest and confident, listen and learn. At different levels of the organisation, people are expected to demonstrate these five behaviours in different ways.

Another interesting feature at Marks & Spencer is the development of an Employee Insight Unit (EIU), which is working to give the organisaton an understanding of how their employees view Marks & Spencer as an employer. The firm has committed itself to delivering 'a great place to work'. The EIU seeks to measure employees' emotional commitment to the workplace in the same way that an already well-established Customer Insight Unit has sought to measure customer loyalty and commitment. The work of the EIU around employment brand can be understood in terms of human capital evaluation because it emphasises the emotional aspects of human capital. For example, in the literature review we discussed human capital in terms of emotional intelligence (EI) and examined the way in which loyalty and commitment were important if employers wanted to maximise the real potential of their human assets. Here, the firm operates an employee feedback survey which provides data on how managers approach their teams. The survey also provides the basis for a more thorough evaluation of employee commitment and morale – something that may be developed in the future.

In effect, then, Marks & Spencer are measuring two different things: (a) the capability of the employees in the organisation through the skills survey, and (b) employees' engagement with the organisation through the Employee Insight Unit. Eventually, it is expected, they will be able to link these two data sets together. As the firm's Director of Organisation Development puts it: 'At some point we should be able to see whether capable people are engaged.' Their approach to human capital evaluation therefore shares similarities with the claim made by David Ulrich that human capital consists of 'competence x commitment' (Ulrich, 1998).

Impacts

The initial skills mapping process will be of value in that it will enable the firm to have a clearer idea of the distribution of its skills and competencies, answering questions on the firm's skill gaps and skill strengths. Importantly, this information will enable the firm to see how the skills of its employees can support its business plans. For example, if the firm was to open a new store, it would be able to make assessments about the type of people that it needs, with what skills, whether it can use existing people, or whether there is a need for recruitment. It is expected that a skills survey of this kind will eventually be incorporated into the performance appraisal system. The information on skills will therefore be collected on a yearly basis and then this information can be fed into the business planning cycle. It is also hoped that information technology can be applied to the process of data collection and analysis.

It is also expected that the information that the firm has generated on competencies and commitment will influence the way in which it targets training and plans for management succession. The generation of data on human capital therefore enables the firm to take a much more strategic approach in its people management.

Drivers
External drivers

The shift toward a system of more strategic human resource management that may lead to the effective evaluation of the firm's human capital was largely a response to external drivers. Marks & Spencer's downturn in the late 1990s has been widely reported in the press. The company share price fell from 664p in May 1998 to less than 180p within two years, and Marks & Spencer's once exceptionally loyal customer base seemed to be turning its back on the firm. However, now on the road to recovery, the firm has placed particular emphasis on the role of HR in supporting the firm's strategic aims and the process of human capital evaluation at Marks & Spencer is a key element in the way the firm has sought to align its people strategy and its corporate strategy.

In November 2001, Marks & Spencer announced a 20 per cent increase in half-year profits. The improvement in profits – from £183.4m last year to £220.3m in the six months to the end of September – was the first increase at the chain store since the spring of 1998. Interviews at the firm reveal that people policies are seen as key to maintaining this turnaround.

Internal drivers

One factor in these developments is a renewed emphasis on strategic planning that incorporates a strategic HR function. This is evidenced in The Cube: a model that outlines the firm's business strategies and how these strategies will be attained through Marks & Spencer's new values, culture and key ways of working. The Cube operates something like a balanced scorecard, with the aim of getting people to think in terms of all six sides of the cube as the company goes through the business planning cycle. The firm has therefore sought to affirm the importance of non-financial issues in the business planning process.

For a retailer like Marks & Spencer, which has suffered greatly in the past from a loss of customer loyalty, it is unsurprising that an emphasis on customer needs is seen as crucial to the delivery of business success. The Cube links together different elements of the business planning process: looking at what customers want, how the firm is going to deliver this, and with what type of people. Information gathering in the form of the work being done through the skills survey or the EIU is key to this process. It is expected that the company will be able to use information gathered regarding its customers and its employees in order to see how specific sets of skills and competencies can help deliver both customer value and at the same time build employee loyalty by making Marks & Spencer a great place to work.

....

AutoCo[1]

AutoCo is a major manufacturing firm engaged largely in the manufacture of automobiles.

Systems and practice

HR practices at AutoCo relate to the measurement of employee competencies and morale in a number of different ways. One example of measuring employee competencies is the system that keeps records on the current skills and capabilities profile of its engineering population. Using this system, it is able identify the people requirements that would be necessary if it were to develop a new product. Such a system enables the firm to see how the capabilities of its current engineering population can be aligned to company strategies in the area of new product development.

More generally, the firm operates a number of different measurement tools that are drawn upon in order to ensure that people-related balanced scorecard objectives are being met. The first of these is the performance review system, which has recently moved away from absolute measures to

1 This is a pseudonym because the firm requested anonymity.

more relative measures of performance, enabling a comparison of employee performance across the firm. The use of 360-degree appraisal also ensures that performance appraisal systems incorporate a high level of feedback. The firm also has tools in place for profiling the quality of its employees in order to build succession planning processes. Employee opinion surveys generate data which has lead to the development of an employee satisfaction index. This satisfaction index is of particular importance to the balanced scorecard in that a target for the employee satisfaction index is incorporated in the scorecard objectives of individual managers.

Impacts

Many of the measurement systems at AutoCo are well established. The employee satisfaction system has been in place for the past 10 years. What is more recent, however, is the alignment of such measurement systems to company strategy. For example, the employee satisfaction information is now seen as one of the ways through which the company can measure its balanced scorecard objectives (with the balanced scorecard system in place for the past 18 months). Information on employee skills and competencies is now being used in a much more focused and strategic way, and not simply as data that are useful only for personal development planning. Thus, management are currently working to incorporate these data into the system which aligns employees' engineering competencies with decisions on new products.

The company has well-established sets of practices that could be understood as human capital management (ie how the firm seeks to develop and retain its human assets). For example, the firm draws upon the data on employee performance,

morale and 360-degree assessment to make decisions regarding employee pay. However, the extent to which the data on employee competencies, performance and morale are employed to evaluate the success of these HR practices is limited. For example, although it is felt that the remuneration system will help to reinforce positive (ie value-creating) behaviours, there has as yet been no attempt to measure this impact.

Drivers

The relatively recent emphasis on the strategic importance of measures of employee performance and satisfaction has been largely a result of changes within the HR function itself. Attempts to measure human capital reflect the way in which the HR function is perceived to be 'getting smarter'. Top management have come to recognise HR as a strategic partner in the business. Within Europe, AutoCo employs over 600 professional HR staff, a population that is equivalent to the workforce requirements for a new model programme. HR runs the balanced scorecard process, and thus it is unsurprising that measures of employee performance, competence and morale are now recognised as important to the attainment of company strategic goals.

Another driver that must be mentioned is the changing business environment. It was shown in the literature review that even for firms producing a tangible product (eg cars), the firm's intangible assets are increasingly being recognised as important. Similarly, at AutoCo the HR director highlighted sales and marketing and more general managerial competencies as just as critical to the firm as its design and engineering competencies. However, it is important not to overstate this emphasis on intangible assets. What is not happening at AutoCo is any attempt to put in

> "*In this company most assets are tangible. But people as an asset is not something that is easily measured. It's measured very easily as a cost because this is very simple to do.*"

place metrics that place a value on their human capital. AutoCo has not conducted a systematic review of those forms of employee competence that are of most value to the business:

In this company most assets are tangible. But people as an asset is not something that is easily measured. It's measured very easily as a cost because this is very simple to do. (HR director)

....

Tesco

As a retailer in the competitive supermarket sector, the business focus at Tesco is highly customer driven. The company states that its core overall purpose is 'to create lifelong loyalty for all our customers'. Employee competencies are viewed as crucial to the achievement of this goal, and thus there is a clear emphasis on understanding the different ways in which employee competencies generate customer value.

Systems and practice

At Tesco the generation of data on employee competencies (especially those that relate to loyalty and commitment) is used in a highly strategic manner. It is necessary, therefore, to give some overview of strategic planning at the firm before we turn to look at how the firm generates data on competencies.

The business is managed strategically through a balanced scorecard system (or 'steering wheel'), people managers at Tesco taking responsibility for ensuring that the people-related goals outlined on the balanced scorecard are achieved. These include goals such as 'living the values of the organisation', and 'winning commitment'. The way in which the HR function seeks to deliver the people-related commitments in its balanced

scorecard is by generating 'hard' data that actually demonstrate the links of the people quadrant to the rest of the steering wheel. This commitment to ensuring good-quality rigorous data in order to measure the achievement of strategic goals has led to the development of a People Insight Unit (PIU) which attempts to measure people issues in all four quadrants of the steering wheel.

The PIU has undertaken work in the area of Key Performance Indicators (KPIs) on people. By establishing KPIs, the PIU is able to demonstrate which people measures are most critical to the attainment of company goals. Through this type of work, the PIU is able to demonstrate to the business how people policies can contribute to business success.

Through the focus on KPIs, the PIU has identified issues surrounding workforce loyalty and commitment as being crucial. The Unit's research into the area of loyalty and commitment has shown that although there are certain functional/ practical reasons behind employee commitment, such as job stability, the emotional aspects of commitment are vital. Through their employee opinion surveys, the PIU has sought to identify the key drivers of emotional commitment. Those themes that were identified included: a) trust and respect; b) support (do people feel valued by their manager?); c) job interests (supporting employee's career development); and d) opportunities (what you get back from the organisation – eg reward). Significantly, these core drivers of emotional commitment were established through a rigorous analysis of employee feedback data.

Impacts

The generation of people data around KPIs by the PIU has the most discernible impact upon the strategic planning process. As part of the annual business planning cycle, an annual people plan is produced which specifies how the company is going to address the KPIs and move them forward. The most significant impact that this process has had is to bring issues of worker loyalty and commitment to the forefront of business planning. The director of the PIU commented on this process by arguing:

If you just deliver for the business, you are going to be totally blind in terms of bringing people with you and gaining commitment.

By maintaining a constant focus on how value is created through people, the PIU is able to demonstrate the value of HR practice (and also show how certain HR initiatives may be of little value). Human capital evaluation at Tesco demonstrates that 'what gets measured gets managed'. The data generated are not simply used to establish whether the firm is meeting strategic goals, but impact upon the day-to-day management practices of the firm. Individual managers will get results from the employee opinion surveys, and these will lead to an action planning toolkit that shows the areas in which that manager needs to develop his or her team, or get more feedback.

Similarly, the data are also used for activities such as succession planning. The firm has used the information on human capital to develop skill profiles which provide a basis for talent spotting. Because Tesco views all employees as vital in securing high levels of customer service, they have rejected the models of succession planning that focus only on the top management population. Talent spotting, therefore, is something that goes on at all levels of the organisation.

Drivers

As a firm operating in the competitive supermarket retail sector, there is a strong focus on building customer loyalty. The work of the PIU has enabled the firm to identify the ways in which customer loyalty can be linked through to employee loyalty and commitment. Thus, human capital at Tesco is not about recruiting and retaining the most talented, innovative individuals, but is about ensuring that the workforce as a whole can be relied upon to deliver the company's strategic goals.

Xerox

Xerox has sought to align its HR practices to overall strategic goals for many years. Thus, the evaluation of human capital here is firmly embedded in an HR function which is regarded as a key strategic partner in the organisation. As with the Tesco case study, we again see a clear focus on creating value for the customer as a key driver behind the role of the HR function. Consequently, some form of human capital evaluation is taking place at all levels of the organisation. As a customer-focused business, it sees little reason in focusing on only the most talented employees, although systems of measuring employee competencies do vary for different workforce populations.

Systems and practice

Strategic management involving the HR department as a key partner has a long history at Xerox. The firm can be seen to be identifying competencies that create value, and using the information to guide reward and career systems.

Yet the firm is also using the notion of employee value and competence in its strategic management systems.

Identifying competencies

There are a variety of techniques in place that could be interpreted as attempts to evaluate the firm's human capital. One of the most obvious examples of this is in the area of attrition costs, where they carry out analyses of the cost of losing employees. For high-performing sales staff, the costs associated with their leaving are very high in terms of lost sales revenue and also the costs of training new people in that role. The firm is now able to estimate the loss of someone in a particular role against lost profit for the business.

More generally, the identification of employee competencies that are viewed as contributing to the value-creating capacity of the firm is being done in different ways for different employee populations. For the sales force, for example, they have developed accreditation and excellence profiles which are definitions of competencies that create maximum value. These profiles are linked to pay, and an employee progresses up the profile by providing evidence that he or she is demonstrating these competencies. Similarly, in the area of the business known as Xerox Business Systems (XBS) – the part of the business that runs print shops or print-related services often based within other organisations – Xerox management have also identified key employee competencies which feed into reward and career systems. Many of these competencies relate to creating maximum customer value through good service and customer awareness. Importantly, given the low-skill low-pay profile of many of the jobs within XBS, the process of identifying value-creating

competencies is not just something that is applied to the most talented, 'business critical' or senior management populations, but is something that is taking place across the firm as a whole.

Aligning competencies to strategy

Some of the techniques for measuring competencies mentioned above have strategic dimensions. For example, using the accreditation and excellence profiles, Xerox are able to correlate the number of people that have reached a certain level of accreditation to the overall performance of the business. Thus it is able to better understand how value is created for the business. On the issue of calculating the cost of attrition, these kinds of business correlations are linked to HR's overall goal of delivering high-performance individuals, which in turn is related to the firm's overall strategic goals.

To understand the wider link between human capital evaluation and strategy, we need to look at the firm's system of total quality management, the Xerox Management Model (XMM). This is an approach that seeks to achieve quality in six business areas: management leadership; HRM; business process management; customer market focus; knowledge and information; and results. Measurement under this model includes a number of people-related issues covering things such as values and vision, managing for results, leadership behaviours, communications and diversity. There are measures associated with each of these areas. Values and vision, for example, is measured through employee feedback surveys. Managing for results is measured through the attainment of performance objectives that are linked to five key aims (cash, revenue, customer focus, cost management, and employee engagement and commitment). The use of measurement tools therefore helps to support the firm's commitment to total quality management.

However, although the XMM enables the firm to be more successful in its core skills and competencies, this is often done in an indirect way. But the firm's HR director felt that overall, compared to other firms, Xerox has made headway in correlating competencies to business success: 'We are getting better at correlating customer value with competency but I think that we do it more implicitly than explicitly.'

Impacts

There are various ways in which the data on employee competencies are being used at Xerox. In XBS, for example, the generation of performance profiles that create value for the business is linked to a system for career progression. By demonstrating certain behaviours and competencies, and undertaking certain types of training, people are rewarded. Thus, work on employee competencies feeds into payment systems, which then act to reinforce positive behaviours.

Drivers

One of the key drivers behind the adoption of more rigorous systems for total quality management (within which the evaluation of human capital is taking place) was the firm's loss of its key patent over 10 years ago. The unleashing of competitive pressures on the organisation paved the way for a more strategic approach to ensuring business performance and total quality management through the XMM.

Norwich Union Insurance (NUI)

NUI is part of the Insurance Group Aviva, which was created out of the merger between CGU and Norwich Union in 2000. Here, the development of various human capital metrics has been driven largely by the impact of merger and the need to ensure that transparent systems of human resource practice were in place after the merger period. As an insurance firm, the skills and competencies that are possessed by certain groups of knowledgeable people – in this case underwriting – are indeed critical to the business. However, a theme throughout the interviews was the importance of evaluating staff competencies throughout the organisation.

Systems and practice
Identifying competencies

The need to develop transparent systems for career development and reward following the merger led to the emergence of a system known as Progression, Performance and Pay (PPP). This system acts to give people information on career development, how their role is defined, how their performance will be measured and managed, and how this links into pay. Sitting alongside the PPP system, training frameworks for identifiable career families are used to identify the sorts of training and development opportunities that can be accessed in order to build and develop individual skills and competencies.

The evaluation of competencies integral to the PPP system is reflected in different ways within distinct business areas of NUI. For example, in operations, they have developed a capabilities matrix, which outlines employees' competence level and knowledge requirements as well as their development needs for specific tasks. In retail, computerised measurement tools ensure that they measure, target and reward the appropriate behaviours to deliver excellent customer service. And in the area known as intermediary business, they have developed an underwriting academy that has developed robust programmes and testing based upon real work evaluation and formal testing. The establishment of the academy illustrates the way that underwriting has been identified as a core skill and is being developed through a vehicle wider than formal training programmes.

Under PPP, there is a clear emphasis on identifying skills and behaviours that drive business success. For example, in relation to career development, the company claims that it is aiming to provide stimulating work that it recognises people for. The way in which it tries to do this is by focusing on the skills and behaviours that are necessary to deliver a performance culture. In particular, there has been an emphasis on not simply reviewing whether results are achieved, but also determining how these results were achieved. The PPP put in place skills and behaviours frameworks that were designed to reflect the firm's 'brand values' of progressiveness, integrity and shared benefit.

Aligning competencies to strategy

These measures of performance and competence are designed not only to guide individuals' career paths, they also link into wider strategic targets. As with many of the other case studies in this report, NUI operates something akin to a balanced scorecard. Business planning at the firm is organised around three strategic goals: profit, morale and service, and there are measures associated with each. As the goal most closely associated with the firm's human capital, morale is

measured using an internal company survey as well as data on short-term sickness absence. The three goals are cascaded down through the organisation via the business planning process, and the aim is for there to be 'line of sight' from every individual's objectives to NUI goals.

It is also important to note that the way in which they measure their human capital is re-evaluated through a goals and objectives programme. This programme evaluates how well the system is working so that the following year they have a better set of measures. Currently, the more strategic dimensions of human capital evaluation are being studied. The company is concerned to discover ways in which it might improve its objective setting, cascade these objectives through the organisation and better align its measuring and reporting tools to the devolved objectives.

Impacts

The evaluation of employee competencies as part of the PPP system has been useful for the firm because it has helped it to forge a common system for dealing with reward, training and career progression across the firm. Drawing upon best practice from both Norwich Union and CGU, PPP has been a highly transparent and visible process so that all the information about the system is available on the firm's intranet site. One benefit of the transparency of the system has been that the firm has seen people moving across the different business functions into equivalent roles. Facilitating the movement of people across the business functions is viewed as very important because, in the past, people would simply leave the business.

The firm is some way from achieving the complete alignment of value-creating employee competencies to strategic goals. The value of certain competencies to the firm tends to be assumed rather than measured. However, because the firm has specified morale as a key strategic goal, it can be seen that PPP has helped to build morale and trust across the organisation.

Drivers

The merger between CGU and Norwich Union was one of the major drivers behind the adoption of approaches to evaluating human capital. There was a need for alignment and consistency in their HR systems and the merger also provided an opportunity to introduce new ideas. One HR director commented, for example, that 'One of the benefits of merger is that you actually do have a chance to start again in terms of policies and you actually have to put new stuff in place.'

But the merger also created serious strains for people management at NUI. During the first year after the merger, the focus of the firm was firmly on the financial goals – the firm had to demonstrate that it was profitable. Consequently, people management concerns suffered. It was against this background that the firm adopted the balanced scorecard approach that incorporated the measurement of employee morale. Since the introduction of the PPP system, measures of employee morale have improved significantly.

The HR function within the firm has been keen to highlight the significance of people to business performance. The HR function at NUI has a great deal of input into company strategy, and in this sense the HR department itself is working to ensure that the evaluation of employee competencies is taken seriously across the business as a whole. To this end, it makes a distinction between HR as a functional activity and broader 'people issues' that relate to how people contribute to the business as a whole.

Motorola

As a large global company employing over 100,000 people, the focus of human capital evaluation at Motorola has been targeted on their leadership population. Motorola aims to build a performance culture through a strategic leadership programme and has established a team responsible for Learning Leadership and Performance (LLP). This unit takes the lead in managing the leadership supply process as well as taking responsibility for organisational learning through the Motorola University, and reviewing performance assessment. Certain elements of human capital evaluation have been built into this strategic focus on leadership, a point that was clearly articulated in the interview:

If you are looking at leadership and you are looking at learning, then you really need to add the other piece, which is how to get a high-performing organisation. Because if you get the right leaders in the right place and you make sure that they have the right skill set, and are rewarded correctly, you can measure how well they are doing.

Systems and practice

A number of different tools are used to assess managerial competencies. First, the Motorola in-house software tool 'Talent-web' is completed by senior managers and other high-potential people. This system goes through work experience and skills developed both inside and outside the firm as well as their aspirations, putting it all in an accessible system. Second, Motorola has developed a leadership assessment model, which is based upon 360-degree appraisal. Called the '4Es+1' (energise, edge, envision, execution + ethics), this model places an emphasis on corporate values in building a performance culture. Finally, an appraisal system is used to rank employees relatively against peers and colleagues. This appraisal system is something that is used across the organisation for all employees, and is a good example of the way in which already available people measurement tools are used for more strategic purposes, such as building a leadership culture.

This process is linked to wider strategic goals through the use of a balanced scorecard. It includes people-related goals such as getting the best people in the best jobs and retaining them. Leadership supply is therefore recognised across the company as a key strategic issue.

Impacts

LLP has aimed to develop a complete leadership supply process. This is an area that is highly relevant to the area of human capital evaluation because it is closely tied to rigorous assessment of managerial competencies and potential. The aim of the system is to create a supply of talent for the organisation, and the process is described as encompassing a 'whole suite of tools' that classify the issue of leadership talent in terms of a number of different stages:

◻ identifying talent

◻ developing talent

◻ rewarding leaders competitively

◻ expecting leaders to deliver

◻ transition (if they are not the right people).

The measurement of leadership potential in turn feeds into a system of reward and development.

One aim is to reinforce positive managerial behaviours. For example, managers have access to on-line information on the skills that they need to develop and can enrol for appropriate training. It should also be noted that this identification of talented individuals is done alongside the identification of the most important jobs at the firm. This means that Motorola management are able to answer the question: 'Are the best people in the most important jobs?'

Drivers

A key external driver behind the development of the leadership supply process at Motorola has been fears regarding the pressure of the market for talented individuals and the need to ensure leadership supply in this context. This thinking is very much influenced by the 'war for talent' ideas originally developed by McKinsey management consultants. The current head of LLP identified leadership as a key issue for Motorola. He saw that in Motorola there was no systematic approach to leadership. In response, he helped to create the Office of Leadership – which reports directly to the CEO – as a separate activity from the University. Although Motorola was not experiencing a loss of key staff, it was felt that it could be a potential problem for an expanding company with an experienced older leadership team. It was also felt that different leadership talents were becoming more important in the new economy. Leadership was seen not simply as being a matter of good technical skills, but also as increasingly encompassing wider business skills (eg finance, marketing and people management skills). Furthermore, benchmarking identified that other organisations had a much more systematic approach in this area.

Internally, we can see that LLP leads the way in driving through a commitment to measurement.

This unit's role is supported by technological developments that enable the firm to operate systems of talent identification and development across a number of different countries. As one respondent indicated: 'You couldn't do global leadership supply, in my view, five years ago. It works because we can do it all on-line.' For a global firm, talent identification is a very difficult process, and software tools such as Talent-web enable the firm to take a high degree of subjectivity out of leadership identification and recruitment by providing a global database of their talent profile, or as one senior manager put it, 'putting data before individual judgement and bias'.

Shell

The oil giant, Shell, has made significant progress in identifying and developing employee competencies. As a vertically integrated firm engaged in a number of different aspects of the oil industry (from exploration to sales and marketing), the firm employs a diverse workforce across the globe. Technological and scientific skills are highly important to the firm, but at the same time commercial skills and customer service are also seen as bringing value to the business.

Systems and practice
Identifying competencies

All major functions have identified well-defined competencies that are seen as critical to performance. These range from the basic-level to higher-level competencies that relate to specific functions of the firm (eg finance, marketing, exploration). They have also identified leadership competencies across the firm – these include, amongst others, 'customer focus', 'valuing diversity', 'commercial capacity', 'communication' and 'global knowledge'.

The firm uses this technique of identifying competencies as part of a formal assessment programme which determines how well competencies are being achieved both within the business and by individuals developing their competencies. This information is then used for the annual development discussion that takes place with employees. This is a tool that reviews employee development over the course of the year. Other evaluation tools include self-assessment tools, systems for peer review, and 360-degree appraisal. These competency evaluation tools generate data that are used by the firm to identify skill gaps. The process of skill-gap analysis is on-going and, because Shell is a global organisation, it is conducted by business and geographical areas.

Aligning competencies to strategy

The identification of these key skills/competencies is part and parcel of how the firm creates strategy. They feel that they are able to identify the skills, behaviours and values that drive success. Again, as with other case studies, there is a clear emphasis on corporate values in delivering results. The HR director comments: 'We want people who share our values and can be educated to share our values.'

At a broader level, strategic planning through the balanced scorecard mechanism is related to a number of people measures. Within the scorecard there are three people metrics: diversity, talent and development of people (learning). Each of these areas is measured against standards that have already been set out through the balanced scorecard process. For example, in measuring talent they want to be able to see if people are meeting their expected potential (ie the expectations that the company had prior to their joining) and make an assessment on this basis. This is an innovative way of identifying talent, which places the focus on building talent rather than fighting the 'war for talent'.

On the issue of development, this is again measured against the criteria that they have outlined in the various development plans that they have in place. They target measurement on things like: are people successfully moving on to new roles? Or, are people mastering the training programmes that they undertake? The firm has rejected, however, some of the more widely recognised measures of employee development, such as number of training days or levels of employee attrition, since this reveals very little about the quality of people development at Shell.

Drivers

At Shell, many of the initiatives for evaluating employee competencies have been in place for decades. As the HR director commented: 'They have a depth, breadth and reach that many firms would envy.' 'Growth and performance' (ie creating value for shareholders) were cited as the primary drivers behind these practices. Shell is a global firm, expanding into new areas of the world. Expansion involves sophisticated human capital investments for both the local people and international staff; hence the need to ensure that these investments are helping to create value for shareholders.

However, certain aspects of the system of evaluating employee competencies are new, in particular the greater emphasis on measurement.

This focus reflects a concern amongst business leaders that 'in business what gets measured gets done'. On the one hand, this discipline in measurement reflects 'a desire to be excellent'. Yet interviews with the HR director revealed that rigorous people measurement systems were also a response to competitive pressures and raised expectations of good practice in this area.

Interestingly, human capital evaluation was linked more broadly to issues of corporate social responsibility. Shell is aware of the changing expectations that society has of business performance (reflected in the concept of the 'stakeholder') which require transparency and rigour in HR practice (and in other areas of business performance). In the interview, it was claimed that practices such as scorecards force them to outline their values and practices and become more transparent in the way they report them. Shell differs from the other case-study firms in this report, because it has sought to link the issue of valuing its employees to a corporate social responsibility agenda. On its website the firm has claimed:

Wherever we work we are part of a local community. We will constantly look for appropriate ways to contribute to the general well-being of the community and the broader societies who grant our licence to operate. (www.shell.com)

However, it is difficult to know whether the use of human capital metrics was driven by this commitment to social responsibility, or whether the firm is incorporating the language of social responsibility into a set of people management practices that were already in place.

> *"The essence of the balanced scorecard is very useful because it forces you to think holistically rather than just think 'Yes, we delivered this programme at that cost."*

BT

At BT, a clear strategic focus on learning and organisational development has not been accompanied by a similar focus on evaluating employee competencies. The interview at BT therefore sought to examine how the firm has approached the issue of human capital evaluation and how it attempts to build the competencies of its workforce.

Systems and processes

BT has a variety of approaches to human capital evaluation. The head of organisational learning commented that:

There are a number of practices ... but none of them are terribly well developed in the way that I'm familiar with in the human capital theories of people like Andrew Mayo. We are some way off that approach to quantifying the value of the capability of people within the business as opposed to simply quantifying the number of people.

However, in certain key areas such as software and network infrastructure it has sought to determine levels of skill capability.

Yet, the BT case study is a complex one because although it cannot be said to be measuring the firm's human capital, it certainly places great value on its human capital. Through an emphasis on learning, the firm aims to build and develop the human capital of the organisation as well as recruit and retain talent. In that sense, BT views the delivery of an effective learning strategy as being more important than the need to measure human capital *per se*.

Some human capital evaluation is involved, however, in the business planning process through the operation of a balanced scorecard. This includes measures of the effectiveness of learning provision provided by the BT Academy and information from employee opinion surveys. As the firm's head of learning put it:

The essence of the balanced scorecard is very useful because it forces you to think holistically rather than just think 'Yes, we delivered this programme at that cost.' It actually forces the issue of looking at the results of things like the annual employee attitude survey in which there are questions about whether you are getting the right sort of development for your role within the business.

Impacts

But there are important examples of how the management of human capital acts to retain talent and sustain company values.

On the issue of talent retention, BT has experienced a loss of key staff in the areas of the business linked to Internet technology. Here it has seen a higher than average labour turnover for key staff. In order to improve employee retention, the company developed a programme called 'Brightstar' at their research lab. Brightstar recognised that there were very talented but very specialised people within the business who were capable of generating ideas that would be useful as a business. The programme enabled these people to form their own start-ups, yet stay within BT. Such initiatives are felt to show that the company is recognising these individuals as valuable to the business.

The impact of the balanced scorecard is seen in areas such as the use of performance-related pay (PRP). When the firm initially moved to introduce PRP, it became aware that it could prove divisive. More recently, it has used a PRP system that aligns with the balanced scorecard approach, such that a proportion of the variable income (the bonus) is linked to team-wide targets, a proportion to the manager's targets and then another proportion to the individual's performance. This is said to produce a team approach that is less divisive and more in tune with company values regarding teamwork.

Drivers

The shift to learning instead of training is part of an attempt to try to make people more responsible for their own career development and to move away from the concept of a definite career path. It is moving to open up opportunities for people across the business and not just confining them to their functional area. This is especially important after a decade of downsizing – over 10 years the company has shrunk from 250,000 to 125,000 people. Downsizing meant that people saw their opportunities for progress diminish since there were fewer jobs, fewer levels in terms of promotion. On top of this downsizing processes, changes in the telecommunications industry have meant that new skills were becoming increasingly important (for example, those associated with Internet service provision).

There were important HR consequences from the downsizing, as the Head of Learning comments: 'It's fair to say that bits of history went with the business. Lots of knowledge went and we've not been particularly good at avoiding that knowledge loss.' Consequently, moves toward better knowledge management have accompanied the shift toward building a learning organisation. The learning part of this is being driven by the Academy, and chief information officers around the business are driving it from the technical and knowledge capture side. So the Academy is working with these people to try to find knowledge solutions that can be used anywhere in the business. However, as yet, BT does not have in place any way of measuring the success of this approach.

BAE Systems

BAE Systems employs 130,000 people across the globe, the majority, 70,000, in the UK. A major change for the business came with the merger of BAE with Marconi two years ago, which effectively repositioned the firm as a systems business rather than a manufacturer of aeroplanes. In this large global company, HR practices are decentralised, group-level HR leaders taking responsibility for key strategic HR issues only. The human capital evaluation process that is discussed for this case study represents the way in which the firm places a strategic focus on leadership competencies.

Systems and processes

Group-level HR takes responsibility for the top 650 management population as well as for certain issues deemed to be of strategic importance. One of the key issues for the company was ensuring that it had an effective leadership supply process and that it could recruit and retain talented business leaders. In this area the firm has developed a highly coherent process for assessing senior managerial (or leadership) competencies and generating outcomes in terms of reward and development.

Under the direction of the HR director and his team, BAE Systems has developed a Performance Centred Leadership (PCL) framework based around five leadership competencies: achieving high performance; focusing on the customer; developing others; continually improving; working together. These are seen as the competencies that a leader needs to possess in order to drive the business forward.

Each of these competencies is further broken down into different behaviours (40 in all). The company seeks to measure the individual's performance against these behaviours and competencies. As with some of the other case studies, we can see that the focus on performance includes certain softer skills relating to how an individual manager sets about achieving his/her targets:

We started by saying it [performance] is about achieving business targets and it's about achieving individual objectives, but it is also about the way in which you do it. So if you just achieve all your business targets and achieve all your personal objectives, but you do it in an inappropriate way – you destroy people in the way that you do it – then you fail the performance criteria. So these five competencies and 40 behaviours are all around driving for an improved performance in an appropriate manner – one that is people-centric. (HR director)

Performance is measured using a variety of different measurement tools, such as 360-degree evaluation, the results of employee opinion surveys, peer assessment, customer feedback and performance review (appraisal). This information is applied to create a forced distribution of the 650 population. Each one is ranked from 1 to 650 and this ranking is then input into decisions on reward, career development, personal development and even whether the individual stays with the firm.

The forced ranking is presented as a colour spectrum: different individuals are graded by a colour, which is supposed to reflect both their performance and their potential. High-performance, high-potential people are either deep or light gold. They expect 5 per cent of the population to be in the top deep gold category; 20 per cent will be in the light gold category; around 60–70 per cent – the majority of the population – will be green (these are solid performers); and the lowest performers will be classified as orange (9 per cent).

There are a number of different training and development outcomes that stem from this ranking (as well as outcomes regarding reward). For those in the lowest category – orange – coaching, mentoring and quarterly performance reviews are then put in place in order to raise each individual's performance. For the deep gold category, a generous personal development fund is provided as well as a specific development programme known as the strategic leaders programme (SLP). The SLP takes 14 months to complete, in a number of different countries. It aims to investigate different strategic mindsets.

The PCL system can be seen therefore to perform a number of functions. First, it is a mechanism through which the firm can pursue performance-centred leadership behaviours across its senior management population. Second, it enables the firm to identify talent and attempt to hold on to that talent. And finally, for the most talented the firm seeks to develop new strategic direction.

Impacts

In terms of impacts, PCL's main benefit is that it brings coherence to leadership planning:

The one thing that's significant about the PCL structure is that, in my view, it is one of the few that combines training and development in a framework with changing the HR policies and procedures that actually determine or drive how an individual is recognised and rewarded. So we've learnt through our previous mistakes that if an organisation is trying to develop its people, very often you find that training departments can do really good work but the old appraisal system is in place, therefore almost forcing people to go back to where they have come from. Or you may get situations where organisations do change their reward mechanisms, but they don't bring training and development in to support this process of change... PCL is designed to attack performance on two fronts. First of all from a development point of view, but also from the point of view of those 'HR' policies and procedures: pay, reward, benefits, methods of evaluating people's performance, and appraisal systems. (Training and development manager)

At the time of the interviews, PCL had been in place for less than 18 months, and this meant that any assessment of the impact of this system was difficult. The company has certain measures – for example, how many personal development plans have been completed since PCL – which indicate that the system is working well. Evaluating the impact of PCL on business success is, however, much more difficult. The key measure of success will be the ability of the business to deliver its business plans. But, as with any people development process, it is very difficult to make correlations back to business success.

Drivers

As mentioned earlier, the merger with Marconi has been a major driver behind PCL in addition to the continued global expansion of the firm. Although the primary reasoning behind PCL was given as the need to improve the performance of the business, a changing organisational context has created an environment within which new ideas and thinking on strategic management can emerge. What has traditionally been a male-dominated engineering firm based in the north-west of England has repositioned itself as a 'systems' business. The Marconi merger in 1999 doubled the size of the business and the firm is now based in eight different countries. It was felt, therefore, that this kind of firm requires a different kind of leader.

The development of a common corporate HR strategy at BAE Systems has given HR the kind of strategic role that was necessary to drive through PCL. Corporate HR has committed itself to a) work collectively together on the 'war for talent', b) work collectively around delivering high-performance leadership, c) work collectively to develop an agile organisation (one that is able to transform itself), and d) see what the actual contribution of the HR function to the business is. All of these elements of the people strategy can be identified in the PCL framework. However, despite the strategic nature of PCL, the HR director was concerned that it would be seen as merely an 'HR initiative' and therefore not taken seriously. It was therefore regarded as very important that PCL was launched not by the HR director but by the CEO.

> **"The products we sell are our people, their reputations in making the right financial decisions – it is all about individual skill, the abilities and capabilities of our people in making money for our clients."**

CityCo[2]

The final case study in this report is an investment bank. The City is one area in which human capital, in the form of individual traders, analysts and fund managers, is highly valued. CityCo's personnel director commented:

It is our staff who create value for our organisation. Our products are all based on human skill and ingenuity – we are not selling cars or new technology. The products we sell are our people, their reputations in making the right financial decisions – it is all about individual skill, the abilities and capabilities of our people in making money for our clients.

The recognition that certain individuals contribute enormously to the value-creating capacity of the firm is reflected in the large bonuses and generous benefits paid to them, as well as various forms of deferred compensation. What are less advanced when compared to other sectors of the UK industry are systems of internal human capital evaluation. Although there is still some way to go to catch up with other sectors, over the past two to three years the firm has introduced 360-degree appraisal for the top 500 people, as well as competency frameworks and significant training and development activity. There is increasing emphasis on these human resource processes, as the firm seeks to broaden the tools it uses to identify, develop and retain its talented people.

Systems and processes

Given that much of the recognition of human capital, particularly of 'fee earners', is still tied to salaries and bonus payments, much of the interview at CityCo focused on how salaries, and the bonus in particular, related to individual performance. What is clear is that although the firm is dependent upon an intangible asset – the judgement and decision-making capacity of individuals – the performance of these individuals is measured in a very tangible way. That is, their performance is measured directly in terms of performance benchmarks achieved, and the quality of client contacts.

Pay at CityCo is structured simply around a basic rate (based on market data obtained through annual surveys and internal relativities) plus a bonus linked to company and individual performance. The individual component for 'fee earners' is based largely on the achievement of performance benchmarks. Although the employees work as teams and have to maintain strong relationships with clients, their success is ultimately determined by the performance of their investment portfolio.

Performance appraisals, which are based upon a discussion of objectives achieved and key competencies demonstrated during the year, will touch upon the softer skills and values the firm believes are important to its success. This is necessary because if people are under-performing they need to understand why this might be and how training or coaching and development might help For 'fee earners', softer 'people' skills – for example, client skills – are viewed as contributing directly to performance, but ultimately the firm looks to the more tangible, that is, financial, aspects of performance when determining what bonuses to pay members of this group.

2 This company requested anonymity, so its name and some of its characteristics have been changed.

> *"We do tend to push one particular button which has got a pound sign next to it – or dollars, or yen – and that's largely because for the people who come to work in the City that's the deal."*

Drivers

Although systematic human capital evaluation is not yet a major feature of HR practice at this firm, it is worth reflecting on the factors that have shaped the current system. In particular, a distinctive challenge is the problem of retaining staff in a highly competitive environment. In this context, while issues of corporate culture do play a role in retaining talent, retention strategy is based very largely on financial incentives. Our respondent commented:

We do tend to push one particular button which has got a pound sign next to it – or dollars, or yen – and that's largely because for the people who come to work in the City that's the deal … You give up your life, work long hours, and have to take some risks; it's relatively high risk and relatively high reward. So if you come to work in the City, you expect certain benefits – basically, you expect to be paid lots of money.

Moves towards a more systematic approach to evaluating human capital have been resisted in the past but are now being made, as the downturn in markets is forcing this company (as well as other City firms) to reassess its position. It is also expected that City firms will eventually be forced to report on the more intangible aspects of their business. The City is a heavily regulated environment, and the Financial Services Authority (FSA) is seeking to ensure that there are systems in place for monitoring and managing performance. Another pressure for change comes from current clients and their agents, who are increasingly asking questions about the people management systems and processes of companies like CityCo as an indicator of organisational health.

Table 3 | Summary of case firms' approach to human capital

Company	Systems and practice	Impacts	Drivers	
			External	Internal
Marks & Spencer	Mapping capabilities through skills survey.	Skills mapping will show how employee skills can support business plans	Downturn in the late 1990s – share price from 664p in May 1998 to 180p less than 2 years later	Renewed emphasis on strategic planning – The Cube
	5 key behaviours			
	Employee Insight Unit			
AutoCo	Records of capabilities profile of engineering population	Used to measure its 'balanced scorecard' objectives		Changes within the HR function itself – 'getting smarter'
	Performance review system	Not used to evaluate the success of HR practices		HR as strategic partner to top management
	Employee satisfaction index			
Tesco	'Balanced scorecard' (KPIs) on people	Impact upon the strategic planning process	Highly competitive	
	People Insight Unit	Annual people plan	Focus on building customer loyalty	
		Skill profiles a basis for talent spotting		
Xerox	Total quality management approach	HR function focused on creating value for the customer	Firm's loss of patent	
	Competence systems vary for different workforce populations	Performance profiles linked to career progression		
	Analyses of exit costs			
Norwich Union Insurance (NUI)	Balanced scorecard	Support reward & development	Merger between CGU and Norwich Union	
	Transparent systems for career development and reward – PPP	Link into wider strategic goals: profit, morale and service		
	Training frameworks			
	'Brand values'			
Motorola	Targeted on their leadership population Learning Leadership and Performance (LLP) team	Leadership supply	'War for talent'	
	'Talent-web' and use of IT	Supports system of reward and development		
	Leadership assessment model			

Company	Systems and practice	Impacts	Drivers	
			External	Internal
Shell	Define basic, higher-level and leadership competencies	Improve leadership capacity	Long-term development	Complements corporate social responsibility goals
	Linked to formal assessment and used to identify skill gaps	Deliver the firm's talent promises	Growth and performance the major drivers	
	Emphasis on corporate values	Implements people strategy	More rigorous measurement systems a response to competitive pressures	
	Balanced scorecard			
	Focus on building talent			
BT	Overcoming reliance on 'headcount' numbers			Decade of downsizing
				Shift to learning v training linked to career ownership development
	In key areas review skill capability			Greater internal mobility
	Focus on learning strategy not evaluation			
	Brightstar programme			
	Balanced scorecard linked to performance-related pay			
BAE Systems	Performance Centred Leadership (PCL) competence-based system provides effective leadership supply for top 650 management population	Provided coherence to leadership planning	Merger with Marconi	Strategic shift from engineering to systems
	Improves identification and retention of talent			Development of corporate HR strategy has given HR strategic role
	Links to training and development outcomes			
CityCo	Less systematic approach to evaluating human capital	Bonuses for retaining staff	Some consultants pay attention to HRM	
	Performance of certain individuals measured through revenue benchmarks			

4 | Analysis and discussion

In reviewing the findings from our case studies, it is important to reflect first of all on the trends that we see evidenced here. Given that this sample of firms was selected on the grounds of their more progressive approach, it is not surprising that in different ways all of these firms were seeking to develop more rigorous approaches to their evaluation of human capital. The reasons for such a development were varied, ranging from the opportunity or challenge provided by mergers and strategic shifts, through to the transfer of good practice by HR professionals.

Many of the existing efforts centred on systems for identifying employee competencies. Such systems afforded the most robust and company-specific means of evaluating human capital. Firms had developed their own criteria of competence, which were linked to the wider business environment they faced, and the values that they sought to apply to that environment. In this way, by developing their own vocabulary and criteria, they overcame some of the problems associated with more generic measures. But while the development and use of competence systems underlines the serious efforts that firms were applying to their human capital, such systems in themselves did not provide a complete solution to the need for evaluation. In some instances, the data generated by such systems provided an input to strategic management, often via the balanced scorecard method of integrating data. In other instances, however, the data on employee competencies were applied primarily within the HR function or to HR-related activities such as pay and appraisal. This suggests that we need to understand not only the kinds of tools that firms are employing to generate data on their employees, but also the context in which those data are used and how they inform other management activities. The value of a human capital perspective here seems to relate to its ability to provide an integrating framework which encompasses a range of issues, and which links the development of competencies to questions of motivation and commitment.

In the remainder of this section we shall explore some of these issues by analysing the data from our case studies.

Organisational context

An important strand in our case studies was the role played by the HR function in the evaluation of human capital. HR involvement was a major feature of our study and, with a few exceptions, the approach to evaluating human capital was driven by HR functions. This meant that these initiatives were unfolding against a wider backdrop of changes in HR functions, including the subcontracting of certain HR tasks such as payroll (as at BAE Systems and BT, for instance). In particular, an important part of the backcloth for these cases was the growing dissatisfaction amongst managers with the effects of performance management systems and, relatedly, the HR function's inability to demonstrate a strategic contribution to the business. In this context, attempts at evaluating human capital were sometimes linked to the HR function's pursuit of greater strategic impact on the business (and greater legitimacy for their own role).

These factors help to explain some of the interactions operating on the evaluation of human capital that we see in our cases. On the one hand, the means of evaluating human capital are often linked to competence-based approaches that have gained wide legitimacy amongst HR functions because they support HR values of objectivity and equal opportunity. On the other hand, HR practitioners are conscious that methods that are too closely associated with their function may not be able to secure legitimacy and commitment from other groups in the organisation. This means that initiatives centred on human capital are carefully decoupled from HR involvement, at least in the way they are presented. In the NUI case, for example, HR managers carefully distinguished between 'HR' and 'people' issues, and several initiatives were explicitly framed in terms of business requirements rather than HR requirements. The role of the balanced scorecard was important here in providing a route by which data about employees could be legitimately considered alongside other forms of data in determining business strategy.

The tension between HR and wider business concerns in the evaluation of human capital seems to have been reflected also in the development of small, specialised units to manage certain aspects of this activity. Thus, we described the development of the PIU at Tesco, the EIU at Marks & Spencer and the LLP at Motorola. These developments highlight the development of new forms of expertise within and between HR and other functions. Such groups are seen as being linked more explicitly to change and innovation and the data that they generate are being developed for wider business reasons which are strategic rather than bureaucratic in nature.

Reporting practices

One significant finding from the study was that none of the case firms was involved in the external reporting of its human capital. Shell is the only one of the sample to call for externally accredited people metrics. None of the firms reported any external pressures to report on their human capital, and none of the initiatives we studied had

an external audience in mind. The consequent focus on internal reporting, therefore, seems to reflect managerial concerns to think more strategically about key HR issues such as recruitment and retention, succession planning, pay, training and development and the purpose of appraisal systems.

The emphasis on internal, managerial reporting also reflects the ability of managers to exploit measurement tools that are already in place, such as competence systems, appraisal systems and employee feedback surveys, and use these to develop a more aggregated understanding of employees' human capital – thereby providing an input to business strategy. On the basis of this kind of evaluation, we found that companies were able to manage their employees' competencies somewhat more effectively. For example, the advantages included:

◘ aligning people strategy to business strategy more closely

◘ evaluating the feasibility of business plans in terms of the levels of employee capability (AutoCo and Marks & Spencer).

◘ identifying skills gaps (Motorola)

◘ reviewing existing HR practices, notably training and development, in the light of new information.

One important development that may help to make human capital evaluation less intractable in future is the widespread use of software-based tools for the generation and storage of information on individual employees. A number of our sample had adopted 'Peoplesoft', and systems such as this were seen as essential to securing accurate and up-to-date information. In firms such as Motorola, BAE Systems and NUI, the development of intranet systems was also seen as important in allowing for interaction between employees and competence systems. Motorola, for instance, has exploited IT most effectively by providing a variety of information flows, including 360-degree appraisals and employee feedback surveys on-line, and then relating that to the training programmes that are most relevant.

Drivers for the evaluation of human capital

Here our study found no single dominant force behind moves towards evaluation. There was no evidence that firms were adopting it simply because it was fashionable, as with other techniques. Rather, there were a number of both internal and external pressures that were prompting managers, mainly HR managers, to develop new practices in this area. These included factors such as:

◘ major organisational changes, such as mergers (NUI and BAE Systems), major competitive threats (Xerox) and a downturn in market share (Marks & Spencer).

◘ developments in HR practice through greater professionalism (Tesco, AutoCo)

◘ the problems of management and succession planning in shifting, increasingly global businesses (BAE Systems and Motorola)

◘ the emergence of HR as a strategic partner (NUI).

Significantly, while these factors helped to explain the emergence of particular approaches at particular times, across all our cases the relative importance attached to the evaluation of human capital seemed to be linked to the industrial context and the nature of the role played by employees. Thus, we found that interest in the evaluation of human capital seemed to be greatest

Figure 4 | Relevance of the human capital perspective

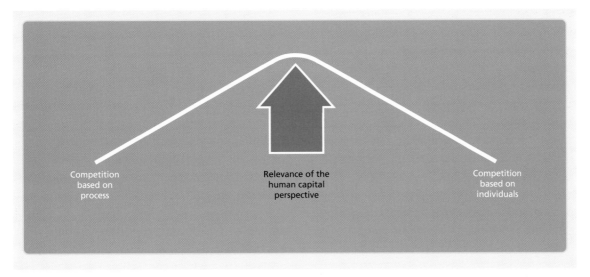

> "Talent was seen as something that applied at all levels, and human capital could be critical anywhere in the organisation."

where employee competencies were a moderately important or ambiguous factor in competitive success. Where such competencies were decidedly secondary to the design and efficiency of the business process there was less need to evaluate them systematically. But equally, where competitive success and financial performance derived directly from the skills of a few individuals, management attention was focused simply on the recruitment and retention of such individuals – the more abstract notion of human capital was seen as having little relevance (see Figure 4).

The war for talent

The area of our sample firms where human capital evaluation was practised most rigorously and with the greatest forensic concern was in the evaluation of small concentrations of individuals who were seen as highly talented and critical to the firm's future. Certain firms perceived themselves as engaged in a 'war for talent', which revolved around identifying, developing and retaining these individuals. There was something of a contrast, however, in the way that firms engaged in this war. Our case firms can be broadly divided into three groups.

First, there were those firms such as BAE Systems, Motorola and CityCo in which the acquisition of specialist knowledge and skills (for example, skills associated with business leadership or financial decision-making) were viewed as crucial to business success. The firm therefore seeks to retain these talented individuals in order to retain key company knowledge and to benefit from the value-creating capacity of these talented people.

Second, and in contrast to the above, were those firms that refused to engage in the war for talent in this way but that sought to build loyalty and

commitment across the workforce as a whole. BT, for example, in a context of downsizing had developed an alternative knowledge- and learning-based approach to talented individuals. It sought to retain them by providing them with new outlets for their talents in the form of the Brightstar venturing business. In addition, BT's systems of knowledge management were designed to retain the knowledge of departing employees. Meanwhile, at Xerox, Tesco and Marks & Spencer, the concern was not with a small concentration of individuals but with the human capital of the workforce as a whole. Talent was seen as something that applied at all levels, and human capital could be critical anywhere in the organisation. This was more the case in firms that had a strong customer focus because it was felt that the provision of a high standard of customer service required building up a loyal and committed workforce. Tesco, Xerox and Marks & Spencer provided examples of firms pursuing these kinds of strategies.

Finally, some of the firms in the study pursued more mixed approaches to talent retention. The most notable case study here was NUI. On the one hand, the firm had identified underwriters as a key talented value-creating population and had strategies in place for retaining this key population. Yet at the same time it had also observed those staff functions associated with the day-to-day operations of the business becoming more critical to the business. Above-average levels of employee attrition in the operations section of the business had meant that the firm saw the retention of talent as an issue even in the less highly specialised areas of the business, such as its call centres.

A focus on the first group of companies is necessary because it was often this group that specifically cited the war for talent ideas as a primary driver (BAE systems and Motorola) and because as firms became more dependent on specialist knowledge and expertise in maintaining competitive advantage, they were more closely identifiable as the kinds of firms normally cited in the war for talent/knowledge economy literature. At Motorola, the influence of the 'war for talent' concept was specifically identified as a driving factor behind the introduction of their leadership supply systems (and thereby their systems for evaluating leadership competencies). Although the firm was not experiencing a loss of key staff, it was felt that as an expanding company with an ageing leadership team this was a potential problem. Furthermore, benchmarking had identified that other firms had a much more systematic approach in this area. Perhaps more significantly, it was felt that different leadership talents were becoming more important in the new economy. Such talents were seen as encompassing not so much technical skills as wider business skills (eg finance, marketing) and people management skills – thus, the company focused its own 'war for talent' on the recruitment and retention of leaders rather than on specific technical skills.

Interviews at BAE systems also revealed the strong influence of the war for talent concept, and again this had translated into a strategic focus on leadership skills. Fears were articulated around the way in which the skills associated with leadership were becoming increasingly generic and therefore transferable. However, this is not to suggest that the firm saw leadership supply and retention systems purely through the lens of the war for talent. Indeed, although the firm recognised that across sectors issues of leadership requirements and capabilities are very similar and that core competencies are the same for leadership across a range of different sectors, there was an explicit

acknowledgement of the importance of organisational values in developing leadership competencies that are firm specific. They have worked to determine the kind of organisation that they want to be and the value set within that (ie the things that they will and will not do) – and these values correspond to how the organisation is led. As the Director, Education and Development put it: 'So there will always be something quite special and unique about the kind of leadership that BAE systems will try and encourage. But competencies of leadership are very similar.'

This acknowledgement that certain skills are highly transferable has meant that certain firms have sought to build systems that build loyalty and commitment. At CityCo this is as basic as paying highly competitive salaries and bonuses in an already highly paid sector. Yet even at CityCo there was an acknowledgement of the role that corporate culture plays in staff retention. At BAE Systems and Motorola, the strategic leadership system, aligned to performance review, pay, training opportunities and career opportunities, is viewed as demonstrating the commitment of the firm to its talented employees, and it is felt that this in turn is rewarded with loyalty and commitment.

The different approaches taken by our case firms can be related to the context and the nature of the human capital they are seeking to manage. The high-tech firms, notably BAE Systems, BT and Motorola, expended considerable effort in securing their key people, as did CityCo. On the other hand, only two of these firms – BAE Systems and Motorola – linked this endeavour to the systematic evaluation of human capital. CityCo felt that the problem of both evaluation and retention resolved itself through the cash nexus. High-level performers were identified through their revenue-

"The development of specialised R&D-type groups suggests
an interest in leveraging human capital information
against strategic objectives in a more direct way…"

generation, and were retained simply by offering salaries high enough to prevent a move to a competing firm. Technical and leadership expertise as at BAE Systems and Motorola may be highly valuable to the firm – hence requiring evaluation and cultivation – but it is less visible and transferable to other firms than investment expertise as at CityCo.

Conclusions

In analysing the experiences of our case firms it has become clear that firms arrive at the issue of evaluating human capital from a variety of directions. Some were stimulated by external pressures and others by internal concerns. Despite their diversity, however, there were also some important common features in their experience – an increasing desire for greater understanding of employee knowledge and skills, coupled, in some cases, with the development of competence systems and the use of IT. The pursuit of more detailed information on employees is not, of course, in itself a major change in HR practice. In some instances, the provision of such information was linked primarily to performance and development objectives, building on existing HR practice. In other areas, however, we can discern signs of a wider business and strategic agenda. The development of specialised R&D-type groups suggests an interest in leveraging human capital information against strategic objectives in a more direct way than conventional HR practices would permit. This is often linked to the development of a balanced scorecard approach which gives human capital factors some access – if still limited access – to the decision-making arena at senior level. This is not to say that the firms in our sample have overcome all of the constraints and problems identified in our earlier analysis. Career mobility, for example, remains a problem for employers, if

not for employees, and it is significant that great attention was being paid, under the martial rubric of the 'war for talent', to issues of retention – a tendency that may, of course, become a vicious circle if it leads to greater competition for a dwindling pool of individuals.

Overall, then, the picture that emerges from our cases is far from monochrome, with a wide variety of home-grown initiatives and systems developing in this area. What seems particularly important about these developments are their links to shifts in the role of the HR function and a wider strategic agenda encompassing new ways of generating and exploiting information on employee competencies. It is these linkages between measuring, reporting and managing human capital which arguably underscore the notion that what we see in our cases properly represents a move towards the evaluation of human capital rather than the development of standard HR practices.

5 | Conclusions

This report has ranged widely over both the theory and practice of human capital. In theoretical terms, we can see that the notion of human capital is most usefully viewed as a *bridging concept* – that is, it spans several different domains of theory and practice. These include the links that it makes between theories of firm performance and models of the management of employees. In terms of practice, moreover, it links HR practices for the development and evaluation of employee competencies to the determination of economic added value.

There remain, however, as our cases demonstrate, major barriers to the development of such a perspective. Management involves the constant balancing of a large number of pressures, both internal and external. Managers seek satisfactory rather than optimal solutions to these pressures (Cyert and March, 1963). It follows that concerted efforts to develop a systematic approach to human capital are likely to arise only where significant pressure is exerted upon the management process. This is less likely to come, for the time being at least, from financial valuations, for the reasons noted above. Nor, in most cases, is it likely to arise from the continuous feedback effects of measures of human capital or targets based on them. As we have already described, such measures tend to be localised to specific firms or to the HR function within firms. They are not, by and large, linked in any serious way to management objectives and accountabilities. If we accept the nostrum that 'what gets measured, gets managed', it follows that, in most firms at the moment, human capital is unlikely to receive the level or kinds of managerial attention that its importance might otherwise deserve.

Given these findings, the use of the term 'human capital' might be seen as inviting critical attention.

A sceptical view might suggest that use of the term is at best managerial rhetoric, and at worst a sinister attempt to turn people into economic units. Against the backdrop of a UK economy where many companies still seem inclined towards low-skill, low-quality strategies (Keep and Mayhew, 2001) the idea of companies' systematically evaluating their human capital might seem hopelessly unrealistic.

On the other hand, against this more critical view our study also provides strong evidence that companies are capable of developing a much more sophisticated understanding of the dynamics of human capital and the extent to which it supports business strategy. This is apparent in the high-tech sector, for instance, where companies concentrate their efforts on the human capital of the most talented managers – the competencies of such groups being undoubtedly perceived as a strategic asset to the firm. But we see it also in firms in the retail sector that have recognised that the collective talent of their workforce amounts to a significant competitive asset, even (or perhaps especially) in a context of tiny profit margins and ferocious cost competition.

We have acknowledged that the context-dependent and dynamic nature of human capital limits the development of generic measures and standards. This is not to say that information flows have no purchase on human capital at all. Rather, as we have seen, information flows need to be embedded in processes of dialogue and exchange which enhance the knowledge of managers, employees and investors as to the value of human capital. Such processes cannot be created by *diktat* or by one group acting independently. They involve bringing together a range of groups inside and outside the organisation. As our case studies show, such processes evolve over time in response to both internal and external pressures and through the interplay between different groups of managers and professional groups. As Leadbeater notes more generally, the problems are not insurmountable. But evaluating intangibles such as human capital involves building a broad coalition of groups and companies which is capable of overcoming the institutional inertia that surrounds existing practices:

Valuing intangibles cannot be resolved within a single academic or professional discipline. It will require a multi-disciplinary approach involving groups such as economists and accountants working together with intellectual property and employment contract specialists. Accounting and market reforms should go hand in hand with legal

and institutional reforms, embracing the operation of markets for capital, labour and intellectual property. (Leadbeater, 2000)

Admittedly, the companies we have described in this report are not typical of UK industry. They were selected to be atypical. Nonetheless, their experience, however provisional or tentative, has begun to outline the kind of virtuous circle that is necessary for change in this area. By linking management to measures, measures to reporting, reporting to management, these companies are beginning to build the credibility, information flows and knowledge necessary to embed a human capital perspective in management practices at both HR and top management level. Indeed, to the extent that increasing numbers of

Figure 5 | Developing the human capital perspective

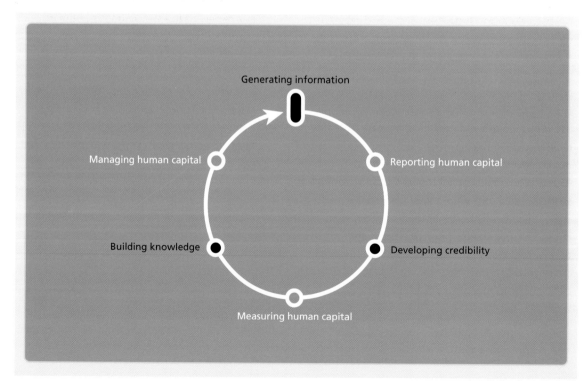

firms seek to evaluate human capital with a view to delivering strategy, it is possible that some new norms of practice may emerge that will provide a platform for measurement and reporting.

We acknowledged earlier, however, that there is no holy grail, no single measure that can adequately reflect the richness of the employee contribution to corporate performance. Our analysis suggests that measures are less important than the activity of measuring, and that is meaningful only in the context of the evolving process described in Figure 5. However, our report also suggests that where such a process develops, it is capable of producing a more coherent and ultimately strategic response to one of the most unknown yet most powerful assets that drive corporate value creation.

Implications for future research

As an exploratory study, our work could only touch on the many far-reaching questions posed by the evaluation of human capital. It is clear from our study, however, that a focus on management practices is crucial if future research is to do more than add to the already extensive theoretical and academic literatures on intangible assets, human capital and HR strategy. Our study shows managers grappling with the problems of evaluating human capital to arrive at more or less workable solutions within their context. Further research in this field should therefore seek to build on and inform leading practices in this area in the following ways.

1. Endeavour to develop a common framework in which different home-grown systems can be located, allowing for greater comparability and transfer of knowledge.

2. Try to identify the major contextual factors that influence the role and importance of human capital in different settings. This would support the development of the above-noted framework by allowing a contingency approach to the challenge, rather than an absolute, one-size-fits-all philosophy.

3. A greater appreciation of the contextual factors that influence the formation and application of human capital would also underpin a more forensic analysis of the usefulness of different systems of measurement and reporting according to circumstances.

4. Finally, research in these areas should be linked to a review of the implications of human capital for management practice, highlighting the interplay between measuring, reporting and managing noted above. In particular, such a review would enable critical scrutiny of the role that HR practitioners play in fostering human capital, and the impact that this has on business strategy and performance.

References

AMIR, E. and LIVNE, G. (2001).

Accounting for human capital when labour mobility is restricted. London: London Business School.

ANNUNZIO, S. (2001).

How to find and develop talent, *People Management* (pp. 64–66).

APPELBAUM, E. and BERG, P. (2000).

High Performance Worksystems: Giving workers a stake. In M. M. Blair and T. Kochan (eds), *The New Relationship: Human capital in the American corporation* (pp. 102–144). Washington: Brookings Institution Press.

ARGYRIS, C. (1977).

Double loop learning in organizations. *Harvard Business Review*, 115–125.

ATKINSON, J. (1984).

Manpower strategies for flexible organisations. *Personnel Management*, 28–31.

BARNEY, J. B. (1991).

Firm resources and sustained competitive advantage. *Journal of Management*, 17, 99–120.

BASSI, L. J., BARUCH, L., LOW, J., MCMURRER, D. P. and SIESFELD, G. A. (2000).

Measuring Corporate Investments in Human Capital. In M. M. Blair and T. A. Kochan (eds), *The New Relationship: Human capital in the American corporation* (pp. 334–382). Washington: Brookings Institution.

BECKER, B. E., HUSELID, M. and ULRICH, D. (2001).

The HR Scorecard: Linking people, strategy and performance. Cambridge, Mass.: Harvard Business School Press.

BECKER, G. S. (1975).

Human Capital : A theoretical and empirical analysis. New York: National Bureau of Economic Research.

BERKOWITZ, S. J. (2001).

Measuring and reporting human capital. *The Journal of Government Financial Management*, 50, 13–17.

BLAIR, M. M. and KOCHAN, T. (2000).

Introduction. In M. M. Blair and T. Kochan (eds), *The New Relationship: Human capital in the American corporation* (pp. 1–27). Washington: Brookings Institution Press.

BONTIS, N. and DRAGONETTI, N. C. (1999).

The knowledge toolbox: a review of the tools available to measure and manage intangible resources. *European Management Journal*, 17, 391–402.

BOYATZIS, R. E. (1982).

The Competent Manager: A model for effective performance. New York: John Wiley & Sons.

BRADLEY, K. (1997).

Presentation. London: Foundation for Performance Measurement.

BURTON-JONES, A. (2001).

Knowledge Capitalism. New York USA: Oxford University Press.

BUTLER, J., CAMERON, H. and MILES, I. (2002).

Grasping the Nettle: Final report of a feasibility study concerning a programme for research into the measurement and valuation of intangible assets. Manchester: CRIC/PREST.

CADDY, I. (2000).

Intellectual capital: recognizing both assets and liabilities. *Journal of Intellectual Capital*, 1.

CARPENTER, M. A., SANDERS, G. W. and GREGERSON, H. B. (2001).

Bundling human capital with organisational context: The impact of international assignment experience on multinational firm performance and CEO pay. *The Academy of Management Journal*, 44, 493–511.

CULYER, A. J. and WISEMAN, J. (1977).

Public Economics and the Concept of Human Resources. In V. Halberstadt and A. J. Culyer (eds), *Public Economics and Human Resources: Proceedings of the International Institute of Public Finance* (pp. 13–29). Paris: Éditions Cujas.

CYERT, R. M. and MARCH, J. G. (1963)

A Behavioral Theory of the Firm. Englewood, N. J.: Prentice-Hall.

DAVENPORT, T. O. (1999).

Human Capital: What it is and why people invest it. San Francisco: Jossey-Bass.

DRAKE, K. (1998).

Firms, Knowledge and Competitiveness, *The OECD Observer* (pp. 24–26).

EDVINSSON, L. and MALONE, M. (1997).

Intellectual Capital. New York: Harper.

FINCHAM, R. and ROSLENDER, R. (2001).

Intellectual Capital Accounting: A review and critique of a management fashion, *17th EGOS Colloquium*. Lyon.

FITZ-ENZ, J. (2000).

The ROI of Human Capital: Measuring the economic value of employee performance. New York: Amacom.

FLAMHOLTZ, E. G. (1999).

Human Resource Accounting. New York: Kluwer Academic Publishers.

GRANT, R. M. (1991).

The resource-based theory of competitive advantage: Implications for strategy formulation. *California Management Review*, 34, 114–135.

GRATTON, L. (1997).

Tomorrow people, *People Management* (pp. 22–27).

GROUP, N. G. R. (1998).

Knowledge Measurement Phase Three: Global survey findings report – Asia, North America, and Europe: Arthur Andersen.

HACKER, C. A. (2001).

How to Compete in the War for Talent. Sanford, Fla: DC Press.

HERMANSON, R. (1964).

Accounting For Human Assets. Michigan: Michigan State University, Bureau of Business and Economic Research.

KAPLAN, R. and NORTON, D. (1996).

The Balanced Scorecard. Boston: Harvard Business School Press.

KEEP and MAYHEW (2001)

Globalisation Models of Competitive Advantage and Skills. SKOPE Research Paper, 22. Coventry: Warwick Business School.

LAVE, J. and WENGER, E. (1991).

Situated Learning: Legitimate peripheral participation. Cambridge: Cambridge University Press.

LAWLER, E. E. and LEDFORD, G. (1992).

A skill-based approach to human resource management. *European Management Journal*, 10, 383–391.

LAZEAR, E. P. (1998).

Personnel Economics for Managers. New York: John Wiley.

LEADBEATER, C. (2000).

New Measures for the New Economy. London: Centre for Business Performance.

LEBLANC, P. V., MULVEY, P. W. and RICH, J. T. (2000).

Improving the return on human capital: New metrics. *Compensation and Benefits Review*, 13–20.

LESTER, T. (1996).

Measuring human capital, *Human Resources* (pp. 54–58).

LEV, B. (1998).

Institute of Chartered Accountants in England and Wales. P. D. Leake Lectures. Oxford.

LINDGREN, R. (2002).

Competence Systems, Viktoria Institute.

LLOYD, T. (1994).

A price on your heads, *Human Resources* (pp. 18–22).

MAYO, A. (2001).

The Human Value of the Enterprise: Valuing people as assets – monitoring, measuring managing. London: Nicholas Brealey.

MAYO, A. (2002).

A thorough evaluation, *People Management*.

McCLELLAND, D. C.

Testing for competence rather than 'intelligence'. *American Psychologist*, 28, 1–14.

MICHAELS, E., HANDFIELD-JONES, H. and AXELROD, B. (2001).

The War for Talent. Boston: Harvard Business School Press.

MILLER, R. and WURZBURG, G. (1995).

Investing in Human Capital, *The OECD Observer* (pp. 16–19).

MURPHY, T. E. and ZANDVAKILI, S. (2000).

Data and metrics driven approach to human resource practices: Using customers, employees and financial metrics. *Human Resource Management*, 39, 93–103.

NORDHAUG, O. (1993).

Human Capital in Organisations: Competence, training and learning. Oslo: Scandinavian University Press.

NORTON (2001)

Building strategy maps. *Balanced Scorecard Report*, 3.2, 1–6.

OATES, D. (1992).

Too Much Round the Middle. *Accountancy: Journal of the ICAEW*, 39–40.

OECD (1996).

Measuring What People Know: Human capital accounting for the knowledge economy. Paris: OECD.

OLVE, N. G., ROY, J. and WETTER, M. (1999).

Performance Drivers: A practical guide to using the balanced scorecard. Chichester: John Wiley.

O'REILLY, C. A. and PFEFFER, J. (2000).

Hidden Value: How great companies achieve extraordinary results with ordinary people. Boston, Mass.: Harvard Business School Press.

PFEFFER, J. (2001).

Fighting the War for Talent is Hazardous to Your Organization's Health. Stanford: Stanford University, Graduate School of Business.

PORTER-LIEBESKIND, J. (2000).

Ownership Incentives and Control in New Biotechnology Firms. In M. M. Blair and T. Kochan (eds), *The New Relationship: Human capital in the American corporation* (pp. 299–333). Washington: Brookings Institution Press.

ROOS, J., ROOS, G., DRAGONETTI, N. C. and EDVINSSON, L. (1997).

Intellectual Capital: Navigating the new business landscape. Basingstoke: Macmillan.

ROSENBAUM, J. E. (1984).

Career Mobility in a Corporate Hierarchy. London: Academic Press.

ROSLENDER, R. and DYSON, J. R. (1992).

Accounting for the Worth of Employees: A new look at an old problem. *British Accounting Review*, 24, 311–329.

ROY, S. (1999).

Managing intellectual capital: the work with the navigator in the Skandia group. *Journal of Human Resource Costing and Accounting*, 4, 59–67.

SACKMAN, S., FLAMHOLZ, E. and BULLEN, M. (1989).

Human Resource Accounting: A State of the Art Review. *Journal of Accounting Literature*, 8, 235–264.

SADLER, P. and MILMER, K. (1993).

The Talent Intensive Organisation: Optimising your company's human resources strategy. London: Economist Intelligence Unit.

SANDBERG, J. (1994).

Human Competence at Work: An interpretative approach. Gothenburg: BAS.

SCRIBNER, S. (1986).

Thinking in action: Some characteristics of practical thought. In R. A. W. Sternberg, R. K. (ed), *Practical Intelligence: Nature and origins of competence in the everyday world* (pp. 13–30). Cambridge: Cambridge University Press.

SPENCER, L. M. and SPENCER, S. M. (1993).

Competence at Work: Models for superior performance. New York: John Wiley & Sons.

STREECK, W. (1989).

Skills and the limits of neo-liberalism: The enterprise of the future as a place of learning. *Work, Employment and Society*, 3, 89–104.

SVEIBY, K. (1997).

The New Organizational Wealth: Managing and measuring knowledge-based assets. San Francisco: Berrett-Koehler.

TEECE, D. (1998).

Capturing value from knowledge assets: The new economy, markets for know-how and intangible assets. *California Management Review*, 40, 55–79.

ULRICH, D. (1998).

Intellectual Capital = Competence x Commitment, *Sloan Management Review* (pp. 15–26).

VANCE, C. (2001).

Valuing Intangibles. London: Centre for Business Performance.

WERNERFELT, B. (1984).

A resource-based view of the firm. *Strategic Management Journal*, 5, 171–180.

WESTPHALEN, S.-A. (1999).

Reporting on Human Capital: Objectives and trends, *OECD International Symposium, Measuring and Reporting Intellectual Capital: Experience, Issues and Prospects.*

YOUNG, A. (1998).

Towards an Interim Statistical Framework: Selecting the core components of intangible investment. Paris: OECD.

YOUNG, S. D. and O'BYRNE, S. F. (2001).

EVA and Value Based Management. McGraw Hill Education.

ZIMMERMAN, E. (2001).

What are employees worth? *Workforce* (pp. 32–36).

ZWELL, M. and RESSLER, R. (2000).

Powering the human drivers of financial performance. *Strategic Finance*, 81, 40–45.

Learning Resources
Centre